HR Manager's Guide to Discipline and Termination Second Edition

Donald B. Jarvis, LL.B.
Carol S. Nielsen, LL.B.
Filion Wakely Thorup Angeletti LLP

31 March 2014

To Ken
All Best Wishes,
Don

CARSWELL®

A cataloguing record for this publication is available from Library and Archives Canada.

ISBN 978-0-7798-2272-0

Printed in Canada by Thomson Reuters.

THOMSON REUTERS

CARSWELL, A DIVISION OF THOMSON REUTERS CANADA LIMITED

One Corporate Plaza
2075 Kennedy Road
Toronto, Ontario
M1T 3V4

Customer Relations
Toronto 1-416-609-3800
Elsewhere in Canada/U.S. 1-800-387-5164
Fax 1-416-298-5082
www.carswell.com
E-mail www.carswell.com/email

About the Authors

Donald B. Jarvis, LL.B.

Donald B. Jarvis, LL.B., is a partner with Filion Wakely Thorup Angeletti LLP. Donald has close to 25 years of experience providing strategic advice to employers to improve their employee relations. His practice involves the representation of management in all areas of labour relations and employment law, including acting as spokesperson at collective bargaining negotiations. He regularly represents both public sector and private sector employers before labour boards, arbitration boards, the courts and numerous employment-related administrative tribunals. He regularly authors articles and papers on topical labour and employment law matters and is a frequent lecturer to both employer groups and labour law practitioners. Donald is certified by the Law Society of Upper Canada as a Specialist in Labour Law and is a Past Chair of the Labour Relations Section of the Ontario Bar Association. Donald currently serves on the Board of Directors of The Advocates' Society.

Carol S. Nielsen, LL.B.

Carol S. Nielsen, LL.B., is a partner with Filion Wakely Thorup Angeletti LLP. Carol practises in all areas of management labour relations and employment law. She has more than ten years of experience working with both public and private sector employers to proactively resolve their human resources issues. Carol devotes a large part of her practice to wrongful dismissals, human rights, pay equity, employment standards, collective agreement interpretation, strategic planning, research and writing. Carol has represented employers before various courts and administrative tribunals, acted as a management nominee in interest arbitrations, and served as the editor of the Ontario Bar Association Labour and Employment Law Section Newsletter.

INTRODUCTION

The administration of disciplinary standards and the imposition of disciplinary penalties are among the most difficult tasks that a human resources professional must face on a day-to-day basis. Each time discipline is imposed, the employer must be prepared to prove that the actual incident(s) of misconduct took place, the imposition of some discipline was warranted, and the particular penalty imposed was just and reasonable in all of the circumstances. If an employer imposes discipline without being prepared to establish the foregoing, the consequences and liability could be substantial.

In a unionized workplace, where the employment relationship is governed by a collective agreement, an employer's decision to discipline or discharge an employee may be challenged through the grievance and arbitration process. In most cases, if an arbitrator finds that there was no just cause for the discipline that was imposed, the arbitrator has the power to rescind or modify the penalty. The arbitrator may even order the reinstatement of a dismissed employee with compensation for wages lost between the dates of dismissal and reinstatement.

In a non-unionized workplace, employees generally do not have access to a grievance and arbitration procedure. However, they may file claims in the courts alleging constructive or wrongful dismissal.

Historically, constructive dismissal has been defined as a unilateral change by an employer of a fundamental term of the employment contract without reasonable notice. However, a 2008 decision of the Ontario Court of Appeal appears to have changed this definition. Even with reasonable notice, any unilateral change to a fundamental term of the employment contract by an employer may amount to a repudiation of the contract. Such an act of repudiation will have consequences depending on how the employee responds to this act of repudiation. Generally, subject to the duty to mitigate, a constructively dismissed employee is entitled to resign and be compensated for damages suffered as a result of the dismissal. Specifically, the employee may claim damages equal to the compensation he or she would have earned during the reasonable notice period. An employee who is discharged without cause, reasonable notice or pay in lieu thereof is said to have been wrongfully discharged. Such an employee is also entitled to damages equal to the amount he or she would have earned during the reasonable notice period. The court determines the reasonable notice period based on such factors as the employee's age, position, salary and length of service.

In addition to the foregoing, any employer that disciplines an employee in contravention of one of the many pieces of legislation governing the employment relationship risks facing serious statutorily imposed consequences.

Separate and apart from legal considerations, a reasonable and transparent disciplinary system should enhance the effectiveness of the workplace. If poorly set up and badly applied, the disciplinary system can undermine the morale of employees and the supervisory authority of front line supervisors, who have preliminary responsibility for investigation and enforcement.

It is clear that employers must be fully aware of the legal principles that govern their rights and obligations with respect to the disciplinary procedure. Every employer should be aware of these principles whether it operates in a unionized or non-unionized setting or, as is frequently the case, in a combination of the two. Equipped with a comprehensive understanding of the relevant legal principles, an employer will be able to effectively utilize the disciplinary procedure to ensure that employees carry out their assigned work in an orderly, efficient, and productive manner.

TABLE OF CONTENTS

About the Authors iii
INTRODUCTION v

PART I: FUNDAMENTALS OF THE DISCIPLINARY PROCEDURE 1

CHAPTER 1: INTRODUCTION TO THE DISCIPLINARY PROCEDURE
1.1 The Purposes of Discipline 1
1.2 Progressive Discipline 2
a) The disciplinary penalties involved in progressive discipline 3
i) Verbal warnings 3
ii) Written warnings 4
iii) Suspensions without pay / final warnings 4
iv) Demotions 5
v) Dismissal 6
1.3 When to Apply the Disciplinary Procedure 6

PART II: THE ELEMENTS OF THE DISCIPLINARY PROCEDURE 9

CHAPTER 2: CONDUCTING A DISCIPLINARY INVESTIGATION
2.1 Introduction 9
2.2 The Purposes of the Investigation 9
2.3 The Timing of the Investigation 10
2.4 Obtaining the Necessary Information 11
2.5 Interviewing Witnesses 12
2.6 Keys to an Effective Interview 13
2.7 The Investigation Report 15

CHAPTER 3: SELECTING THE APPROPRIATE DISCIPLINARY PENALTY
3.1 Factors Influencing Discipline / Discharge 19
a) The collective agreement or employment contract 20
b) Applicable policies and procedures 20
c) The severity and nature of the offence 21
d) Previous cases and consistency 21
e) The employee's previous record and the doctrine of culminating incident 22
f) The employee's explanation 23

g) Provocation 23
h) Additional relevant circumstances 23
3.2 Statutorily Prohibited Motives (Ontario Legislation) 24
a) The *Labour Relations Act, 1995* 25
b) The *Employment Standards Act, 2000* 26
c) The *Ontario Human Rights Code* 30
d) The *Occupational Health and Safety Act* 35
e) The *Workplace Safety and Insurance Act, 1997* 35

CHAPTER 4: DEALING WITH SPECIFIC TYPES OF EMPLOYEE CONDUCT
4.1 Introduction 37
4.2 Leaving Work Without Permission 37
a) Personal Emergency Leave 38
b) Emergency Leave, Declared Emergencies 39
c) Reservist Leave 40
d) Family Medical Leave 40
e) Organ Donor Leave 41
4.3 Lateness 41
4.4 Dishonesty 42
4.5 Sabotage / Property Damage 48
4.6 Fighting / Violence in the Workplace 48
4.7 Insubordination 54
4.8 Sexual and Discriminatory Harassment 55
4.9 Conflict Of Interest 57
4.10 Off-Duty Conduct and Criminal Convictions 58
4.11 Breaching Company Rules 63
4.12 Absenteeism 64
a) Innocent absenteeism 64
b) Culpable absenteeism 69
c) Employment Standards Leaves 73
4.13 Performance Issues 73
4.14 Last Chance Agreements 76

CHAPTER 5: ELEMENTS OF THE DISCIPLINARY / DISCHARGE LETTER
5.1 Introduction 81
5.2 Disciplinary Record 81
5.3 The Infraction 81
5.4 The Disciplinary Penalty Being Applied 81
5.5 Available Employee Support / The Positive Aspect of the Disciplinary Penalty 82
5.6 Serving Notice of Future Discipline 82

CHAPTER 6: SAMPLE DISCIPLINARY LETTERS

6.1 Introduction 85
6.2 Sample Letters 85
a) Suspension for fighting 85
b) Warning for unauthorized absence from work 86
c) Suspension for unauthorized absence from work 86
d) Suspension for theft 87
e) Dismissal for damaging company property 88
f) Warning for failure to adhere to safety policies 88

CHAPTER 7: THE DISCIPLINARY AND DISCHARGE MEETINGS
7.1 Introduction 91
7.2 Tone 91
7.3 Clarity and Completeness 92
7.4 Witnesses 92
7.5 Timing 93
7.6 Location 93
7.7 The Offer to Resign 93
7.8 Following Up After the Disciplinary Meeting 94
7.9 The Termination Meeting 95
7.10 After A Dismissal 97
a) Personal items 97
b) References 97
c) Other employees 98
d) Post-discharge obligations 98
7.11 Maintaining Employee Disciplinary Records 106

PART III: ADDITIONAL CONSIDERATIONS 109

CHAPTER 8: COLLECTIVE AGREEMENT CLAUSES
8.1 Introduction 109
8.2 Sample Clauses 109
a) Just cause 109
b) Timeliness 110
c) Presence of a union representative 110
d) Issuing reasons 111
e) Reviewing personnel files 111
f) Sunset clauses 112
g) Non-discrimination clause 113
h) Deemed termination 114

CHAPTER 9: POTENTIAL DAMAGES ARISING FROM THE TERMINATION OF EMPLOYMENT
9.1 Overview 119

9.2 Unionized Employees 120
9.3 Non-Unionized Employees 121
a) The *Employment Standards Act, 2000* 121
i) Notice of termination / termination pay 121
ii) Severance pay 122
b) The common law 123
i) Bad faith discharge 125
c) Damages for loss of benefits during the period of reasonable notice 127
i) Vacation pay 127
ii) Pensions 127
iii) Group benefit plans 128
9.4 Aggravated and Punitive Damages 132
a) The Law Following *Wallace* 132
b) The Law Following *Keays* 133

INDEX 137

Part I: Fundamentals of the Disciplinary Procedure

Chapter 1: Introduction to the Disciplinary Procedure

1.1 — The Purposes of Discipline

There are three widely recognized purposes of discipline:

- to rehabilitate the employee;
- to deter other employees from engaging in behaviour similar to that of the offending employee; and
- to ensure that the employer maintains the confidence and respect of other employees.

Of these three purposes, rehabilitation should be the foremost consideration when an employer imposes a disciplinary penalty. Through the effective application of the disciplinary procedure, many employees can be encouraged to correct their behaviour to conform to the employer's expectations.

Deterrence is also a legitimate goal of discipline. An employer that does not intervene when an employee repeatedly engages in misconduct risks having other employees view the employer's inaction as a form of condonation. Such perceived condonation may lead to increased misconduct by other employees, as well as disrespect for managerial authority.

With respect to maintaining the employees' confidence and respect, employees generally notice the poor performance of one of their colleagues long before any manager or supervisor. This observation is often made when employees are forced to assume greater responsibility to compensate for the poorly performing employee. In such circumstances, a failure by the employer to act can lead to a sense of unfairness among employees which may negatively affect morale and ultimately performance.

A fourth, although not universally recognized purpose of discipline, is punishment. At the very least, punishment should be intended as a positive rather than a negative exercise designed to support one of the other three purposes of discipline.

A final purpose of discipline should be to support the possible termination of employment where an employee cannot or will not be rehabilitated.

1.2 — Progressive Discipline

One of the key aspects of an effective disciplinary procedure in a unionized workplace is adherence to the principle of progressive discipline. The principle of progressive discipline arises out of the theory that an employee should not be severely disciplined unless he or she has been adequately warned that the behaviour in question is inappropriate. Thus, progressive discipline involves imposing a less severe disciplinary penalty for a first offence and gradually increasing the severity of the penalty for further offences. With the imposition of each disciplinary penalty, the employee is warned that further misconduct may result in a more severe disciplinary penalty. An employee who is subject to progressive discipline will know that after receiving a warning he or she may receive a suspension, and following that he or she may be discharged for failure to correct the unacceptable conduct. Progressive discipline thus affords employees repeated opportunities for rehabilitation. If an employee ultimately fails to rehabilitate himself or herself after being subjected to a series of increasingly severe penalties, the employer may rely on the employee's failure to improve as evidence that the employee cannot be rehabilitated. The employee's dismissal may then be justified on the basis that he or she cannot be rehabilitated.

In a non-unionized workplace, employers must ensure that the application of progressive discipline does not result in the constructive dismissal of an employee. Where an employer unilaterally alters a fundamental term of employment, the employee may consider himself or herself to have been constructively dismissed and claim damages for wrongful dismissal. In general, courts have held that a reasonable and fair application of progressive discipline will not give rise to a constructive dismissal. However, an unwarranted or unreasonable disciplinary measure may constitute a fundamental breach of the employment contract. Factors including the seriousness of the disciplinary measure, the circumstances in which the discipline was applied, and the existence of any relevant workplace policies or express terms of the employment contract will be considered. Generally, the likelihood of a disciplinary measure giving rise to a constructive dismissal increases with the severity of the measure. For this reason, employers should be particularly cautious when imposing a severe disciplinary penalty such as a suspension without pay. However, some case law has suggested that progressive discipline may be equally as applicable and appropriate in the non-unionized setting as in the unionized workplace.

a) — The disciplinary penalties involved in progressive discipline

i) — Verbal warnings

The first stage of progressive discipline is often the verbal warning. In some workplace cultures, a verbal warning may not necessarily be considered to be a formal disciplinary penalty. Despite its name and informal nature, some written record should be kept that a verbal warning has been issued. The purpose of a verbal warning is to influence an employee in a non-coercive manner. A verbal warning also demonstrates the employer's good faith in attempting to correct an employee's behaviour.

Many employers place too much reliance on verbal warnings. Employers are often more comfortable verbally warning an employee than imposing a formal disciplinary penalty. However, it is important to recognize that a verbal warning may have a lesser impact on an employee than a more severe disciplinary penalty. Depending on the circumstances, an employee may wonder how serious the matter truly is if the employer did not even deem it worthy of a written warning. In many cases, only a more formal disciplinary penalty, such as a written warning, will impress upon an employee the seriousness of the misconduct, encourage the employee to reflect on the employer's dissatisfaction with his or her behaviour, and ideally contribute to his or her rehabilitation.

Verbal warnings should not be used in situations involving human rights or health and safety offences. If there are recurrences, the weak response of a verbal warning could potentially increase liability.

ii) — Written warnings

The written warning is the least severe formal disciplinary penalty that an employer may impose on an employee, at least where the verbal warning is not considered to be formal discipline. It consists of a written notice to the employee that sets out the misconduct giving rise to the warning and any earlier verbal warnings relating to the misconduct. The written warning should also indicate that further unacceptable behaviour could lead to more serious disciplinary penalties. In this respect, the written warning clearly signals to the employee that the disciplinary procedure has been invoked.

An advantage of written warnings over verbal ones is that they evidence the employer's efforts to warn and rehabilitate the employee. An employer may rely on this evidence to support subsequent, more severe, discipline.

The use of written warnings that are properly prepared after due consideration of the relevant circumstances can also reduce the risk of "spur-of-the-moment" verbal admonitions of employees. Spur-of-the-moment responses to employee misconduct are generally not very effective in fulfilling the purposes of discipline. Furthermore, a spur-of-the-moment response may preclude a subsequent more serious response. It is only appropriate to issue a single penalty for each incident of misconduct. If an employee is issued a verbal warning by the supervisor, the employer may not be able to issue a more severe penalty (e.g. a written warning or suspension) once the employer has had an opportunity to reflect further on the events.

iii) — Suspensions without pay/final warnings

A suspension without pay is the most severe disciplinary penalty, short of discharge, available to employers. The length of the suspension should reflect the severity of the offence and the employee's disciplinary record.

Generally, suspensions should be from one to five days. A series of increasingly long suspensions may be issued. For example, a one day suspension may be followed by a three day suspension and finally by a five day suspension together with a final warning.

One of the main objectives of a suspension is to encourage the employee to reflect on his or her behaviour and recognize the seriousness of his or her actions. This purpose does not ordinarily require a suspension of more than five days. However, an extended suspension could be appropriate where an employee has committed an offence that merits dismissal, but due to extenuating circumstances the employer does not wish to proceed with a dismissal. In such a situation, a more lengthy suspension without pay may be effective.

In a non-unionized setting, employers should be aware that a suspension, particularly an unwarranted or unjustified disciplinary suspension, might constitute constructive dismissal. This possibility is minimized if the employment contract or a clearly communicated policy allows for a suspension. As previously stated, however, some courts have suggested that progressive discipline, including suspensions without pay, may be an entirely appropriate response to culpable conduct on the part of the employee and, accordingly, may not amount to constructive dismissal.

Typically, before discharge takes place, the employee should be given a "final warning" that if there is further disciplinary conduct of any kind whatsoever, he or she will be subject to immediate discharge or summary dismissal. Such final warnings may be included in a letter imposing a suspension without pay. Obviously, such warnings are the final step in progressive discipline before discharge. Such action is designed to clearly notify the employee that his or her continued employment is now in jeopardy and that previous efforts to correct the employee's behaviour have all been without success. In the face of progressive discipline and a "final warning" both courts and arbitrators will be loathe to second guess the employer's action of discharge following any kind of culminating incident.

iv) — Demotions

Another serious disciplinary penalty that an employer may consider is the disciplinary demotion. In a unionized context, employers wishing to effect a disciplinary demotion, should ensure that management's right to demote is not specifically limited by collective agreement provisions dealing with, for example, seniority, discipline, or transfers. It is much easier to succeed with a temporary demotion than one that is indefinite or permanent.

In a non-unionized workplace, a disciplinary demotion may be imposed where an employer has just cause to dismiss an employee, but wishes to retain the employee's services. If the demotion is justified in this manner, the employee will not likely be able to establish that a constructive dismissal occurred. In certain circumstances, such as where the contract of employment expressly provides for demotions, a demotion may be imposed even where the employee's actions are not quite sufficient to meet the standard of just cause. Generally, if no reduction in pay accompanies the demotion, it is less likely that a constructive dismissal will be established. However, the internal prestige or status and responsibility associated with the positions are also important considerations.

v) — Dismissal

The disciplinary dismissal permanently severs the employment relationship between the employer and the employee. It may be justified by a single serious offence or an accumulation of lesser offences pursuant to the doctrine of culminating incident (see Chapter 3, *infra*).

1.3 — When to Apply the Disciplinary Procedure

An employer should apply the disciplinary procedure if an employee fails or refuses to correct unacceptable workplace behaviour after the employer has engaged non-disciplinary measures or the employee's behaviour warrants an immediate invocation of the disciplinary process. For example, when work performance issues are involved, an employer should give the employee a performance review or evaluation setting out the details of the unsatisfactory performance. If the employee does not immediately demonstrate an honest effort to improve, the employer may elect to implement the disciplinary procedure. Progressively severe disciplinary penalties may then be imposed as necessary to correct the employee's behaviour.

Discipline may not necessarily be appropriate when an employee is simply incapable of achieving the required standard. Poor performance that is due to inability or a lack of knowledge or training should be addressed by the employer through "non-disciplinary" measures such as re-assignment or re-training, but not discipline. Similarly, innocent absenteeism that is due to illness or injury should be handled through a non-disciplinary attendance management programme.

When the disciplinary procedure has achieved its principal objective, the rehabilitation of the employee, the employer may return to non-disciplinary methods of employee management to further improve the employee's performance. If the employee resumes the improper conduct, the employer should return to the disciplinary procedure.

A severe disciplinary response may be required in cases of serious misconduct, notwithstanding the absence of any earlier discipline. For instance, a severe disciplinary response may be appropriate where the health and safety of an employee or the protection of the employer's property is in jeopardy.

PART II: THE ELEMENTS OF THE DISCIPLINARY PROCEDURE

CHAPTER 2: CONDUCTING A DISCIPLINARY INVESTIGATION

2.1 — Introduction

While it is generally unpleasant for an employee to receive a disciplinary penalty, it is often equally unpleasant for the manager or supervisor who is responsible for administering the penalty. An understanding of the various elements that comprise the disciplinary procedure can increase managers' and supervisors' comfort levels when administering discipline. It can also enhance the overall quality of the disciplinary procedure.

The first step in the disciplinary procedure is the disciplinary investigation. When an employer determines that a situation may require the application of the disciplinary procedure, it should immediately begin a disciplinary investigation.

2.2 — The Purposes of the Investigation

A thorough investigation serves five important purposes.

First, a thorough investigation will put the employer in the best possible position to select an appropriate disciplinary penalty.

Second, a thorough investigation will provide an employer with a basis for defending any disciplinary penalty that is imposed. When an employee challenges a disciplinary penalty, the burden will generally be on the employer to establish that the discipline was for just cause. Consequently, it is extremely important for the employer to thoroughly investigate all of the relevant circumstances before administering a disciplinary penalty.

Third, a thorough investigation indicates to the employee in question that the employer is attempting to obtain all of the relevant information and is not going to take action based on mere speculation or supposition. This knowledge may reassure the employee that his or her situation is being assessed in a fair and objective manner. If the employee knows that the employer has acquired all of the relevant information prior to the imposition of discipline, the employee and, where applicable, the union may realize that the employer can establish strong grounds for the action taken. The employee and the union may, therefore, be more inclined to accept the employer's ultimate decision.

Fourth, a properly conducted investigation will include the creation or gathering of relevant records or reports. Such documents may refresh the memories of witnesses who are called upon to testify before a court or an arbitrator. Hearings often do not take place until months or even years have passed after the disciplinary penalty was imposed. Memories inevitably fade in the intervening period. At a hearing, a witness is generally allowed to refer to any notes that were made contemporaneously with the event in question as an aid to his or her recollection. In addition, if there is a conflict in the testimony of two witnesses as to what actually occurred, the evidence of a witness who can bolster his or her testimony by referring to notes made at the time of the occurrence will often be considered more reliable.

Finally, in any hearing, the manager or supervisor who conducted the investigation and made the decision to impose the discipline may be one of the employer's principal witnesses. Being able to establish that a thorough investigation was conducted will greatly enhance the credibility of this witness. An employer cannot afford to have the credibility of its investigator called into question, especially where his or her evidence is contradicted in a material respect by the employee who was disciplined or by other witnesses.

2.3 — The Timing of the Investigation

In all cases, potential disciplinary issues should be investigated and dealt with as expeditiously as possible. The more quickly an investigation is completed, the greater the reliability of witnesses' recollections. A prompt response also reassures employees that the issue is being taken seriously. Without such reassurance, employees may feel frustrated by a real or perceived failure of the employer to act. In cases of misconduct involving co-workers (e.g. fighting, harassment), an expeditious investigation minimizes the emotional strain on employees and decreases the likelihood of permanent damage to relationships within the workforce. Finally, an employer that unnecessarily delays an investigation may be considered to have condoned or accepted the misconduct.

In some cases, it may not be possible to complete a thorough investigation prior to the imposition of remedial action. For instance, if a night shift employee comes to work under the influence of alcohol, the supervisor in charge may not have any alternative but to send the employee home immediately. The recommended procedure in such cases is to advise the employee that he or she is suspended pending completion of the investigation, after which a final decision will be made. Depending on the circumstances and the likelihood that discipline will be imposed, the suspension may be with or without pay. Generally, however, it is preferable to suspend with pay pending the outcome of the investigation. This minimizes the likelihood of a constructive dismissal claim by a non-union employee and, in all cases, minimizes the scope for arguing that any discipline imposed after the investigation is precluded by the doctrine of double jeopardy. As in the criminal context, in the employment context an employee can only be disciplined once for each act of misconduct. An argument can be made that even a suspension with pay is a disciplinary penalty that prevents an employer from issuing more severe discipline (e.g. discharge) after the conclusion of the investigation. Accordingly, it is critical that the suspension be clearly identified, preferably in writing, as being "pending the outcome of the investigation". The investigation should then be completed at the earliest possible opportunity. The investigation may disclose that the employee was intoxicated because of a death in the family or some other mitigating circumstance, which may have some bearing on the discipline to be imposed.

2.4 — Obtaining the Necessary Information

In the course of the disciplinary investigation, the employer should gather all relevant information and record it in writing. The types of information that may be relevant include the following:

- the time and location of the incident giving rise to the proposed disciplinary response;
- details regarding the incident and the events leading up to it;
- names of all witnesses;
- statements made by the employee in question, the manager or supervisor, and all witnesses; and
- copies of all documents relating to the incident (e.g. correspondence between the parties, written rules, regulations and policies, disciplinary records, previous grievances and settlements, minutes of meetings, medical reports, and negotiation records).

All the facts upon which an employer intends to rely when disciplining an employee must be verified for their accuracy. Although such verification takes time, it is far better to discover any "surprises" with respect to the facts during the investigation than at a later stage of the disciplinary procedure.

2.5 — Interviewing Witnesses

One of the most important aspects of a disciplinary investigation is the interviewing of witnesses.

In general, all witnesses with any degree of involvement in the events giving rise to the discipline should be interviewed. Witnesses may include employees, managerial personnel, individuals who are not employees (e.g. customers), and the individual who is the focus of the investigation. Meeting with all witnesses will best enable the employer to determine what actually happened and whether any disciplinary penalty is warranted. Furthermore, if the discipline is challenged, the conduct and results of the investigation will assist the employer in establishing that the discipline was justified. For example, if at a hearing into the matter a witness attempts to change or embellish his or her story, a prior inconsistent statement by the witness may be put to him or her and used to impeach his or her credibility.

Information from an individual who did not personally witness the event but rather obtained relevant information from another individual is considered hearsay. Hearsay and rumours should not be relied upon even if the employer believes them to be accurate.

It is advisable to obtain witnesses' accounts as soon as possible after the event in question. As time passes, people's memories fade and their recollections may be influenced by the comments of others. In addition, employees will often be reluctant to cooperate with an employer's investigation against a fellow employee. However, immediately after an event, an employee who is offended or embarrassed by a colleague's behaviour may be more eager to cooperate.

Sometimes, the final witness who will be interviewed in an investigation is the very person who may be the subject of discipline. This way, he or she will be able to respond, or at least be given an opportunity to respond, to all other information that has been gathered in the investigation. Ultimately, in every investigation, the person who is alleged to have engaged in any kind of wrongdoing should be given an opportunity to respond to and be confronted with the evidence against him or her. This is essential to ensure procedural fairness.

It is very important to keep the investigation meeting (i.e. what happened?) separate from the discipline meeting (i.e. what is the consequence?), even if the separation between the two meetings is nothing more than a coffee break. Procedural fairness demands that final decisions regarding disciplinary action are not made until *after* the fact finding investigation has been completed.

2.6 — Keys to an Effective Interview

The following are the basic steps that an employer should follow to ensure an effective interview:

- Conduct interviews separately to prevent witnesses from being influenced by the stories of other parties. A witness may also be more forthcoming in the absence of other employees.
- Ensure that the right people are in attendance at the interview. In a unionized setting, employees should generally have a union representative present, especially if the employee who is being interviewed is likely to be the subject of discipline. The applicable collective agreement may also mandate some form of union representation. The employer should have two persons present at the interview: the interviewer (who may also make notes) and a second person whose role is to carefully record what is said.
- In a unionized setting, ask the union representative if he or she has any procedural objections to proceeding with the interview.

This question will ensure that any procedural issues may be dealt with immediately. Often, the union representative will waive a procedural irregularity and agree to proceed with the interview immediately. Any such agreements should be recorded in the interview notes.

- Allow the witness to first relay the facts in his or her own words. If necessary, prompt the witness to complete certain parts of the story. If the witness is having difficulty remembering certain events, it may be advisable to provide him or her with relevant documents in order to refresh his or her memory. Once the witness has explained what happened, the interviewer may use questions to explore aspects of the witness's statement more fully. Ask the witness to specifically respond to statements from other parties and to explain any inconsistencies between his or her story and the observations made by the other parties.
- Fully explore any explanations or excuses provided by the witness with additional questions.
- Give (or at least show) copies of any documents used at the interview to the witness and the union representative.
- Give the witness an opportunity at the end of the interview to provide any further information. It is generally advisable to delay answering any of the witness's (or union's) questions until this time.
- At the conclusion of the interview, advise the witness that there may be further interviews if the investigation raises additional questions.
- Make detailed notes of what is said at the interview. The notes should include details such as the date and time at which the interview took place, who was present, and what documents, if any, were exchanged. At the conclusion of the interview, the witness should be asked to review the notes to ensure their accuracy and sign them. If the witness refuses to sign the notes, the interviewer should ask him or her to read the notes and verbally confirm their accuracy. The interviewer should then attach a note indicating that the witness verified the accuracy of the notes, or otherwise specifying what the witness had to say about the notes.

- After the interview, follow up on any explanations or excuses given by the witness that you were unable to fully explore during the interview. If necessary, another interview may be conducted to allow the witness to respond to questions that arise as a result of the follow up investigation.

2.7 — The Investigation Report

Once the investigation is complete, the employer should prepare an investigation report. The report should contain the relevant facts and should include copies of the relevant documents. While such a report will generally only take a short time to prepare, it may be invaluable in later justifying the disciplinary action taken. A sample outline for an investigation report is found on the following pages.

DISCIPLINARY INVESTIGATION REPORT	
Employee's name: Date & time of incident: Location of incident:	Employee's supervisor: Date of report: Report prepared by:
SUMMARY OF EVENTS BASED ON EMPLOYEE'S ACCOUNT	
WITNESSES (Include additional contact information for witnesses who are not employees)	
Name: Position:	Name: Position:

Interviewed on: Interviewed by: Individuals present at interview:	Interviewed on: Interviewed by: Individuals present at interview:
Name: Position: Interviewed on: Interviewed by: Individuals present at interview:	Name: Position: Interviewed on: Interviewed by: Individuals present at interview:
WITNESSES WHOSE ACCOUNTS COULD NOT BE OBTAINED	
Name: Position: Reason account could not be obtained:	Name: Position: Reason account could not be obtained:

SUMMARY OF EVENTS BASED ON WITNESSES' ACCOUNTS

Summarize witnesses' accounts including differences between the accounts

RELEVANT DOCUMENTS ATTACHED TO THIS REPORT

1.
2.
3.

4.
5.

CONCLUSIONS

CHAPTER 3: SELECTING THE APPROPRIATE DISCIPLINARY PENALTY

3.1 — Factors Influencing Discipline/Discharge

After the investigation has been concluded and all necessary parties have been consulted, the employer must decide upon the appropriate course of action. Specifically, the employer must determine whether a disciplinary penalty is required and, if so, select the appropriate penalty. In undertaking this process, the employer should ensure that the disciplinary procedure is applied consistently. Any inequality in treatment will frustrate employees and lead to resentment of the employer's disciplinary practices. Such inconsistency may also constitute a basis for challenging the discipline at arbitration.

In addition to ensuring consistency, an employer must select a disciplinary penalty that is neither too lenient nor too severe. If the penalty is too lenient, it will not serve as a satisfactory deterrent to other employees or fulfill any of the other purposes of discipline. If the discipline is too severe, the employer may later be forced to reach a compromise with the employee or the union. In a unionized workplace, an arbitrator may also rescind or modify the discipline. If the employer dismissed an employee, the employer may be required to reinstate the employee and even pay damages. Rescinding or modifying a disciplinary penalty may undermine employees' confidence in the manager or supervisor who imposed the penalty and compromise the effectiveness of the disciplinary procedure.

The selection of the proper disciplinary penalty is, therefore, an important decision that must only be undertaken after a consideration of a number of factors. The key factors that must be considered are:

- the collective agreement or employment contract;
- applicable policies and procedures;
- the severity and nature of the offence;
- previous cases and consistency;
- the employee's previous record;

- the employee's explanation;
- provocation; and
- any additional relevant circumstances or mitigating factors.

a) — The collective agreement or employment contract

In unionized environments, the relevant provisions of the collective agreement should be kept in mind at all times. The collective agreement may set out important time limits for investigating and imposing discipline. The collective agreement may also set out the appropriate penalty for a particular offence or dictate the procedure to follow in imposing discipline. Additional examples of limitations and requirements that are often set out in collective agreements include:

- time limits with respect to disciplinary interviews;
- the requirement for the attendance of a union representative at an interview or at the time discipline is imposed;
- restrictions on the use of an employee's disciplinary record;
- limitations on temporarily suspending employees; and
- special requirements with respect to the format of disciplinary notations.

In a non-unionized workplace, the applicable employment contract should similarly be considered.

b) — Applicable policies and procedures

Employers should review workplace policies and procedures to determine if they apply to the conduct in question. Employers should keep in mind, however, that not every breach of a policy or procedure will justify discipline.

In a unionized context, the breach of a policy or procedure that does not constitute part of the applicable collective agreement will not necessarily constitute just cause for discipline. To ensure valid reliance upon such a policy or procedure, the employer must have clearly notified employees of the policy or procedure and the consequences of its breach. The employer must also ensure that the policy or procedure is reasonable and consistent with the applicable collective agreement. Finally, the policy or procedure must be applied in a fair and non-discriminatory manner.

In non-unionized settings, courts will similarly scrutinize employers' rules to determine whether they are reasonable, whether they are incorporated into the employment contract, and whether they justify discipline in the circumstances.

In both unionized and non-unionized workplaces, it is generally advisable to have employees sign acknowledgements that they have read, understood and agree with applicable policies. Such acknowledgements will increase the likelihood of discipline based on a breach of policy being upheld.

c) — The severity and nature of the offence

Conduct that could give rise to just cause for discipline could range from arriving at work a few minutes late to theft or sabotage. For minor offences, the discipline imposed should also be minor. For example, a verbal warning may be an appropriate response to a first incident of relatively minor misconduct. Continued problems, however, should be subject to progressively more severe disciplinary penalties.

Serious offences, such as theft or assault, may properly require the imposition of severe discipline, including discharge, after only one offence. However, if mitigating factors are present (e.g. length of service or remorse), an arbitrator may not uphold the discharge or a court may determine, in a non-union case, that there is not cause for dismissal and the employee is entitled to damages. For this reason, it is important to always carefully review the facts of each case before selecting a disciplinary penalty.

d) — Previous cases and consistency

Another important factor is the manner in which the employer has dealt with similar offences in the past. Consistency in the imposition of disciplinary penalties gives employees an indication of what to expect. Previous cases also provide the employer with some guidance in determining the appropriate penalty. In addition, an employee may claim discrimination if he or she is disciplined for conduct that has not previously been the subject of discipline. Such an allegation of discrimination could be especially troublesome if there are human rights overtones to the case. If an employer repeatedly fails to discipline employees for a particular type of misconduct and then, without warning, singles out one employee and disciplines him or her, an arbitrator or court may find the discipline to be unreasonable.

When relying on past disciplinary practices, the employer should consider all circumstances of the earlier incidents, including factors such as length of service and work history.

e) — The employee's previous record and the doctrine of culminating incident

When determining the appropriate penalty, the employer should consider the following elements of the employee's record:

- the length of time the employee has been with the employer;
- the nature of any previous disciplinary incidents involving the employee;
- the separation in time between previous discipline and the current situation;
- the severity of any discipline previously imposed;
- the connection between the past disciplinary record and the misconduct in question; and
- any positive steps taken by the employee before or after the incident to reduce the possibility of a recurrence.

For example, a long-term employee with no disciplinary record should not be subject to the same degree of discipline for an isolated act of insubordination as a short-term employee who had previously been disciplined for insubordination.

Employers should be aware of the doctrine of the culminating incident. The doctrine of the culminating incident provides that where an employer can establish what amounts to a final incident of disciplinary misconduct, the employer is entitled to rely on the employee's disciplinary record to justify the penalty being imposed. In other words, even if an employee commits a relatively minor offence, the employer is entitled to review the employee's entire work record (to the extent that it is allowed by the collective agreement) and impose discipline, or even discharge, based upon that record. The employer may be required to demonstrate that the employee was aware of and had an opportunity to challenge all of the previous disciplinary incidents being relied upon. Additionally, the employer should refer to the previous events being relied upon in the letter of discipline or discharge.

Some collective agreements contain provisions referred to as "sunset" clauses or "cleansing" provisions. A sunset clause requires references to an employee's disciplinary penalties to be removed from his or her record after a certain time period has elapsed. As such, a sunset clause will limit the extent to which an employer can rely on an employee's previous disciplinary record. Even in the absence of a sunset clause, the weight put on an employee's previous record will generally vary according to the amount of time that has elapsed since the disciplinary events referred to in the record.

f) — The employee's explanation

Where an employee offers a reasonable explanation for his or her conduct, discipline should not be imposed unless the explanation is not believed or does not justify the conduct. Where an employee can show that he or she was genuinely unaware that the conduct would lead to discipline, an arbitrator or court may find that the discipline was not justified or ought to be reduced. Of course, some incidents attract discipline regardless of whether the employee honestly believed that no misconduct had occurred.

g) — Provocation

An arbitrator or court may find a severe disciplinary penalty to be excessive if a supervisor or another employee provoked the employee's misconduct. For example, in cases involving assaults on forepersons, where it is shown that the foreperson was at least partially to blame, the penalty of discharge has often been reduced. A foreperson or other managerial employee may provoke an employee by, for example, physically or verbally assaulting the employee.

h) — Additional relevant circumstances

Any and all circumstances that may be relevant to an assessment of the employee's actions should be considered. Such circumstances will often have a significant impact upon whether an arbitrator or court finds the employer's actions to be reasonable and justified.

For example, disciplinary incidents are often partially the result of personal circumstances over which an employee has limited control. As an arbitrator or court will consider such circumstances when assessing an employer's disciplinary response, an employer should also consider them before deciding on an appropriate penalty. Consequently, during an investigation, an employer should be alert to any potential mitigating circumstances, such as marital problems or medical problems involving the employee or the employee's family members. Similarly, genuine remorse expressed by the employee may be considered as a mitigating factor.

Employers should also consider the context in which the disciplinary response is issued. For example, if an employee recently received a favourable performance review, it will be more difficult for the employer to justify a dismissal based on poor performance. Although many employers utilize overly positive reviews and congratulatory notices to encourage employees to improve their performance, the effect of such practices on the disciplinary procedure should be considered. As a general rule, employers are best served by issuing fair and accurate evaluations as well as follow up evaluations when an employee's performance undergoes a dramatic change.

The employee's status as a union official may also be important in some cases. For example, if the employee is alleged to have instigated an unlawful walkout, the fact that the employee is a union official may be an aggravating factor.

Employers should be aware that the doctrine of "double jeopardy" may prohibit imposing two penalties for the same incident. This doctrine does not prohibit an employer from imposing more than one disciplinary penalty or remedial measure with respect to one offence (e.g. in response to a motor vehicle infraction, an employer may suspend the employee and require the employee to take a remedial driving course). Instead, double jeopardy prohibits an employer from imposing a particular penalty or penalties with respect to an offence and then, several days later, escalating the penalty or changing it.

3.2 — Statutorily Prohibited Motives (Ontario Legislation)

When determining whether an employee's misconduct merits a disciplinary response, an employer must ensure that all relevant statutory requirements are observed. For example, there are several employment-related statutes in Ontario that prohibit an employer from disciplining or discharging an employee based on certain prescribed grounds. Where an employer disciplines an employee in contravention of one of these statutes, the discipline may be overturned and the employer may face penalties.

Where statutory consideration comes into play, the employer should be prepared to fully justify the discipline on the proper grounds and establish that no improper purpose for the discipline exists.

a) — The *Labour Relations Act, 1995*

The *Labour Relations Act, 1995*, S.O. 1995, c. 1, Sch. A (the "*LRA*") establishes certain "unfair practices" in which parties, including employers and unions, are prohibited from engaging. Specifically, employers are prohibited from interfering with employees' rights pursuant to the *LRA*. For example, an employer is prohibited from refusing to employ or discharging a person because he or she is a member of a union or is exercising any other rights pursuant to the *LRA*. Employers are also prohibited from using threats or penalties to compel an employee to refrain from becoming or to cease to be a member or officer of a union. Employers are similarly prohibited from seeking to compel an employee not to exercise any rights pursuant to the *LRA*.

Consequently, an employer must not discipline an employee for exercising any right pursuant to the *LRA*, including:

- participating in a union organizing campaign;
- participating in a lawful strike; or
- participating in the collective bargaining process.

Where an employer is party to a collective bargaining relationship with a union or an employee or group of employees is seeking to establish such a relationship and the employer disciplines or discharges an employee contrary to the *LRA*, the employer may be subject to proceedings before the Ontario Labour Relations Board (the "OLRB").

The *LRA* places the burden of proof on the employer in any complaint alleging that a person was discharged, refused employment, discriminated against, threatened, coerced, intimidated or otherwise dealt with contrary to the *LRA* with respect to his or her employment, conditions of employment, or opportunity for employment. This burden of proof must be satisfied on the civil standard of a balance of probabilities.

Generally, to establish that the discipline or other adverse treatment of a union supporter does not violate the *LRA*, the employer must satisfy the OLRB that the action in question was in no way motivated by the employee's trade union activity or any anti-union sentiment or "animus". The employer is not required to establish just cause for any discipline imposed. Even if there is a legitimate business reason or just cause for the discipline at issue, a violation of the *LRA* will be established if the employer was motivated, even if only in part, by anti-union considerations.

To determine whether an employee's discipline was motivated, in whole or in part, by anti-union animus, the OLRB considers the totality of the circumstances, including the following factors:

- the existence of union activity and the employer's awareness of such activity;
- any previous anti-union conduct by the employer;
- the nature of the employer's investigation into the employee's alleged misconduct;
- the credibility or plausibility of the employer's explanation for the discipline;
- the objective reasonableness of the discipline; and
- the timing of the discipline.

If the OLRB finds that the employer violated the *LRA*, it may order the employer to cease doing or rectify the act forming the subject of the complaint. If an employee has been dismissed, the OLRB may order the employer to reinstate the employee with or without compensation. In certain rare circumstances, where an employer contravenes a provision of the *LRA* or an order of the OLRB, the employer may be found guilty of an offence and on conviction may be liable to a fine of not more than $25,000 for each day of the contravention.

b) — The *Employment Standards Act, 2000*

The *Employment Standards Act, 2000*, S.O. 2000, c. 41 prohibits employers from intimidating, dismissing, or otherwise penalizing an employee or threatening to do so because the employee exercised or attempted to exercise a right pursuant to the *Employment Standards*

Act, 2000. Employers are specifically prohibited from disciplining an employee for any of the following:

- asking the employer to comply with the *Employment Standards Act, 2000*;
- making inquiries about the employee's rights pursuant to the *Employment Standards Act, 2000*;
- filing a complaint pursuant to the *Employment Standards Act, 2000*;
- giving information to an employment standards officer;
- participating or intending to participate in a proceeding pursuant to the *Employment Standards Act, 2000*; and
- taking, intending to take, or being or becoming eligible to take one of the leaves provided for pursuant to the *Employment Standards Act, 2000*.

The rights pursuant to the *Employment Standards Act, 2000* referred to above include rights related to:

- payment of wages;
- hours of work;
- overtime pay;
- minimum wage;
- public holidays;
- vacation with pay;
- leaves of absence such as pregnancy leave, parental leave, and emergency leave; and
- termination and severance of employment.

Where an employer disciplines an employee contrary to the *Employment Standards Act, 2000*, an employment standards officer or an arbitrator may order that the employee be compensated for any loss that he or she incurred as a result of the contravention. If the employee is dismissed contrary to the *Employment Standards Act, 2000* provisions dealing with leaves of absence or certain other prescribed provisions, an employment standards officer or arbitrator may order that the employee be reinstated.

Notably, with respect to unionized employees, the *Employment Standards Act, 2000* is enforceable at arbitration as if it were part of the collective agreement. An employee who is covered by a collective agreement will not be able to file a complaint with the Ministry under the *Employment Standards Act, 2000*. The prohibition against unionized employees filing complaints with the Ministry applies even if the employee is not a member of the trade union. However, it is program policy that during a lawful strike or lockout (or afterwards if the workplace has shut down without a new collective agreement having been entered into), bargaining unit employees are entitled to file claims under the *Employment Standards Act, 2000* for contraventions or failures to comply with the *Employment Standards Act, 2000* that occurred during the lawful strike or lockout.

The *Employment Standards Act, 2000* specifically provides that an employee who is represented by a trade union that is or was a party to a collective agreement is bound by any decision of the trade union with respect to the enforcement of the *Employment Standards Act, 2000* under the collective agreement. Accordingly, a unionized employee is bound by any decision of the union on the issue of whether or not to proceed with the employee's grievance or any other decision of the union with respect to enforcement (e.g. decisions regarding what remedies to seek or what evidence to adduce at arbitration). While an employee is bound by a decision of the union with respect to his or her grievance, the *Employment Standards Act, 2000* expressly provides that the employee has the right to file a complaint against the union for unfair representation under section 74 of the *Labour Relations Act, 1995*.

Despite the general prohibition against unionized employees filing complaints regarding the *Employment Standards Act, 2000* outside of arbitration, the Director of Employment Standards may permit an employee to file a complaint and may direct an employment standards officer to investigate it "if the Director considers it appropriate in the circumstances". The circumstances under which such discretion would likely be exercised are extremely limited.

With respect to non-union employees, they have a general right to file complaints under the *Employment Standards Act, 2000* with respect to alleged breaches of the legislation. However, an employee who files a complaint under the *Employment Standards Act, 2000* with respect to an alleged failure to pay wages or an alleged failure to comply with employment standards requirements regarding benefits plans may not commence a civil proceeding with respect to the same matter. Similarly, an employee who files a complaint under the *Em-*

ployment Standards Act, 2000 alleging an entitlement to termination pay or severance pay may not commence a civil proceeding for wrongful dismissal if the complaint and the proceeding would relate to the same termination or severance of employment.

Parallel provisions exist for employees who commence civil proceedings. Specifically, an employee who commences a civil proceeding with respect to an alleged failure to pay wages or failure to comply with the *Employment Standards Act, 2000* regarding benefit plans may not file a complaint under the *Employment Standards Act, 2000* with respect to the same matter or have such a complaint investigated. Similarly, an employee who commences a civil proceeding for wrongful dismissal may not file a complaint alleging an entitlement to termination pay or severance pay or have such a complaint investigated if the proceeding and the complaint relate to the same termination or severance of employment.

Despite the foregoing restrictions, an employee who has filed an employment standards complaint may commence a civil proceeding with respect to the same matter if he or she withdraws the employment standards complaint within two (2) weeks after it is filed. Although there is nothing in the *Employment Standards Act, 2000* that provides for an extension of the two (2) week time limit, a court has inherent jurisdiction to extend a limitation period in circumstances that warrant it. In *Scarlett v. Wolfe Transmission Ltd.*(2002), 2002 CarswellOnt 3917, 21 C.C.E.L. (3d) 69 (Ont. S.C.J.), the Ontario Superior Court of Justice granted an extension of the time limit. In that case, the defendant brought a motion to dismiss the plaintiff's wrongful dismissal claim on the basis that he had not withdrawn his earlier *Employment Standards Act* claim within the mandated period. At the time of bringing the employment standards claim, the plaintiff was unrepresented. He later retained legal counsel who commenced his civil suit. The court found that the motion should be dismissed as there was no real prejudice in allowing the plaintiff to proceed with his wrongful dismissal suit and a "gross miscarriage of justice" would occur if he were denied his day in court. The Court was obviously influenced by the equities of the situation and the traditional view that the matter should be decided on its merits.

c) — The Ontario *Human Rights Code*

The Ontario *Human Rights Code*, R.S.O. 1990, c. H.19 provides that every person has a right to equal treatment with respect to employment without discrimination because of:

- race;
- ancestry;
- place of origin;
- colour;
- ethnic origin;
- citizenship;
- creed;
- sex;
- sexual orientation;
- age;
- record of offences;
- marital status;
- family status; or
- disability, which includes:
    - any degree of physical disability caused by bodily injury, birth defect or illness;
    - a mental disorder; and
    - an injury or disability for which benefits were claimed or received pursuant to the *Workplace Safety and Insurance Act, 1997*, S.O. 1997, c. 16, Sch. A.

Where an employer disciplines an employee contrary to the *Human Rights Code*, the employee may file a complaint with the Ontario Human Rights Tribunal (the "Tribunal"). As of June 30, 2008, all human rights complaints must be filed directly with the Tribunal. Previously, complaints were submitted to the Human Rights Commission, which could investigate the complaint and, if it is appropriate, refer the complaint to a hearing before the Tribunal. Under the new "direct-access" model, the Tribunal expects that the number of complaints, now referred to as "applications," will increase from 100 to 150 per year to approximately 3000 per year.

Under the new system, the time limit for filing a claim has been extended from 6 months to 12 months. As such, an applicant must file the application within 12 months of the date on which it is alleged that discrimination occurred. Once an application is accepted by the Tribunal for processing, the Tribunal will send a copy of the application to the named respondent. Within thirty-five (35) calendar days, the respondent must respond to the application by filing with the Tribunal a completed response. The Tribunal will then send a copy of the response to the applicant. Within fourteen (14) days after the response is sent to the applicant, the applicant may submit a reply to any new matters raised in the response. The reply must be delivered to the Tribunal and the other parties.

Applicants and respondents are required to provide more information on their respective application and response forms than what was required under the old system. Both parties must list the witnesses and documents that they believe are important to their case and must also list documents that are needed but are in the possession of other individuals.

Under the *Human Rights Code*, the Tribunal is permitted to disclose copies of applications and responses to the Ontario Human Rights Commission. The Tribunal may permit the Commission to intervene in an individual application "on such terms as the Tribunal may determine having regard to the role and mandate of the Commission." The Commission may also intervene as a party to an application if the applicant consents to the intervention.

If the Tribunal finds that an employee's right was infringed, the Tribunal has broad remedial powers to address breaches of the *Human Rights Code*. The Tribunal has the authority to award such remedies as damages for lost wages, damages to compensate for the right not to be discriminated against, reinstatement and promotion, as well as to order the implementation of polices, procedures and training. The Tribunal also has the authority to award damages for mental distress. Under the old system, an award for mental distress was limited to $10,000. Under the new system, there is no longer a monetary cap on the amount of damages that can be awarded for mental distress.

In the unionized setting, the *LRA* expressly confers upon arbitrators the power to interpret and apply human rights legislation. This power was also conferred upon arbitrators pursuant to the 2003 decision of the Supreme Court of Canada in *Parry Sound*. Now, an arbitrator may have jurisdiction to apply the *Human Rights Code* not merely in situations where the arbitrator finds a sufficient connection or nexus between the *Human Rights Code* and collective agreement — which appeared to be the law prior to this recent decision of the Supreme Court of Canada. Additionally, in certain circumstances, an arbitrator may consider the *Human Rights Code* as an aid to interpreting a collective agreement.

For non-union employees, as a result of the 2008 amendments to the *Human Rights Code*, Ontario courts now have the power to determine in a proceeding if a party's rights under Part I of the *Human Rights Code* have been infringed and to award a remedy for the infringement. Subsection 46.1(1) of the *Human Rights Code* states as follows:

> If, in a civil proceeding in a court, the court finds that a party to the proceeding has infringed a right under Part I of another party to the proceeding, the court may make either of the following orders, or both:
>
> 1. An order directing the party who infringed the right to pay monetary compensation to the party whose right was infringed for loss arising out of the infringement, including compensation for injury to dignity, feelings and self-respect.
>
> 2. An order directing the party who infringed the right to make restitution to the party whose right was infringed, other than through monetary compensation, for loss arising out of the infringement, including restitution for injury to dignity, feelings and self-respect.

The *Human Rights Code* also makes it clear that an alleged violation of the *Human Rights Code* does not, by itself, create a civil cause of action. Subsection 46.1 (2) states as follows:

> Subsection (1) does not permit a person to commence an action solely on an infringement of a right under Part I.

To claim a remedy for a *Human Rights Code* violation in the courts, a plaintiff must assert some other cause of action, such as wrongful or constructive dismissal. The alleged *Human Rights Code* violation, however, may arise from the same set of facts that are pleaded to support the main cause of action.

The addition of section 46.1 to the *Human Rights Code* is consistent with the Supreme Court of Canada's earlier ruling that a breach of the *Human Rights Code* does not create an independent tort of discrimination at common law: *Bhadauria v. Seneca College of Applied Arts & Technology*, [1981] 2 S.C.R. 181, 1981 CarswellOnt 616, 1981 CarswellOnt 117, 124 D.L.R. (3d) 193 (S.C.C.). However, the addition of section 46.1 has made it clear that in the context of another civil proceeding, courts in Ontario have the power to award a remedy where the *Human Rights Code* has been violated.

The remedial powers of the courts are set out in subsection 46.1 (1), *supra*. Specifically, a court may award monetary compensation to a plaintiff, whose rights under the *Human Rights Code* have been infringed, including compensation for injury to dignity, feelings and self-respect. A court may also order a non-monetary award, namely "restitution for injury to dignity, feelings and self-respect."

It is unclear how the courts will interpret and apply their power to order "restitution" under the *Human Rights Code*. The Supreme Court of Canada has stated that "the word 'restitution' implies that something has been given to someone which must be returned or the value of which must be restored by the recipient": *Peel (Regional Municipality) v. Canada*, [1992] 3 S.C.R. 762, 1992 CarswellNat 659, 1992 CarswellNat 15, 98 D.L.R. (4th) 140 (S.C.C.). "Restitution" has also been considered by the Tribunal under the former *Human Rights Code*, which provided the Tribunal with the power to direct a party to make restitution where a *Human Rights Code* infringement had been found. In *Fuller v. Daoud* (2001), 2001 CarswellOnt 5337 (Ont. Bd. of Inquiry), the Tribunal considered the definition of "restitution" and stated the following:

> ... Restitution is an equitable remedy. That restitutive power allows the Board to restore a complainant to her or his original position before the loss or injury occurred; or to place a complainant in the position he or she would have been in, if the breach had not occurred. Restitution includes the act of restoration including restoring anything to its rightful owner; the act of making good or giving the equivalent for any loss, damage or injury one sustains; or indemnification. Restitution may take on different forms depending on the nature and legal context of the breach (see Black's Law Dictionary, 6th ed.).

In *Wedley v. Northview Meadow Co-operative Homes Inc.*, 2008 CarswellOnt 1748, 65 C.C.E.L. (3d) 292 (Ont. Human Rights Trib.), the Tribunal observed that pursuant to its power to order restitution,

> ... Tribunals have ordered both personal remedies, such as promotion or reinstatement in employment, and public interest remedies, such as the establishment of workplace anti-discrimination policies and staff training.

While it is not uncommon for the Tribunal to order personal remedies such as reinstatement, courts have traditionally refrained from ordering that a plaintiff be reinstated to his or her employment. At this point, it is uncertain how the courts will apply the power to order non-monetary restitution under section 46.1 of the *Code*. It is likely that individuals seeking non-monetary personal remedies as well as public interest remedies will pursue their human rights claims through the Tribunal process rather than the courts. However, in respect of individuals who are seeking only monetary awards, employers may expect claims for damages for any alleged violation of the *Human Rights Code* in civil claims for wrongful or constructive dismissal.

An individual is prohibited under subsection 34(11) from filing an application to the Tribunal in respect of a *Human Rights Code* violation under the following two circumstances:

1. a civil proceeding has been commenced in a court in which the person is seeking an order under section 46.1 with respect to the alleged infringement and the proceeding has not been finally determined or withdrawn; or
2. a court has finally determined the issue of whether the right has been infringed or the matter has been settled.

An individual who has commenced civil proceedings for wrongful or constructive dismissal would not be prevented from filing an application with the Tribunal if the individual does not also claim civil damages for an alleged *Human Rights Code* violation. Employers may minimize the likelihood of individuals commencing applications before the Tribunal after settling their wrongful dismissal actions by having the individuals sign comprehensive and carefully worded releases at the time of settlement.

d) — The *Occupational Health and Safety Act*

The *Occupational Health and Safety Act*, R.S.O 1990, c. O.1 (the "*OHSA*") prohibits an employer from:

- dismissing or threatening to dismiss an employee,
- disciplining or suspending or threatening to discipline or suspend an employee,
- imposing any penalty on an employee, or
- intimidating or coercing an employee

because the employee acted in compliance with the *OHSA* or sought enforcement of the *OHSA*. For example, an employer may not discipline an employee for refusing work where he or she has reason to believe that the work (i.e. the physical condition of the workplace or any equipment, machine, or thing that the employee is to use or operate) is likely to endanger himself, herself, or another employee.

An employee (both union and non-union) who believes that he or she has been disciplined contrary to the *OHSA* may file a complaint with the OLRB. On an inquiry by the OLRB, the employer bears the burden of proving that it did not violate the *OHSA*. Specifically, the employer will be required to show, on a balance of probabilities, that the disciplinary action in question was not motivated, even in part, by the worker's compliance with or enforcement of the *OHSA*. If the OLRB finds a violation of the *OHSA*, it has similar remedial powers as in the case of a violation of the *LRA*.

e) — The *Workplace Safety and Insurance Act, 1997*

The *Workplace Safety and Insurance Act, 1997*, S.O. 1997, c. 16, Sch. A requires employers to cooperate in the early and safe return to work of employees who sustain injuries arising out of or in the course of employment. Specifically, there is a statutory duty to re-employ employees in certain circumstances. The re-employment obligation applies to an employee who has been unable to work as a result of a workplace injury and who, on the date of the injury, the employer had employed continuously for at least one year. Once the employee is medically able to perform the essential duties of his or her pre-injury employment, the employer must offer to re-employ the employee in his or her pre-injury position or an alternative position of a nature and at earnings comparable to the employee's pre-injury position.

If an employer re-employs an employee and then terminates his or her employment within six months, the employer will be presumed to have not fulfilled its statutory obligations. This is a rebuttable presumption. The employer will be required to demonstrate, on a balance of probabilities, that the termination was not related to the employee's injury. If an employer fails to fulfill its statutory obligations, the Workplace Safety and Insurance Board may levy the prescribed penalty on the employer.

Chapter 4: Dealing with Specific Types of Employee Conduct

4.1 — Introduction

Every instance of employee misconduct must be considered on an individual basis taking into account all the relevant circumstances, including all the factors set out in the preceding chapter. Nevertheless, general observations can be made with respect to the proper approach for dealing with certain types of employee misconduct.

The following categories of conduct form just cause for discipline and, in appropriate circumstances, may justify discharge.

4.2 — Leaving Work Without Permission

Except in emergencies such as cases of injury or sudden illness where no supervisor is readily available, an employee is not entitled to leave work without obtaining permission from a member of management. An employee who leaves work without such authorization or legitimate excuse may be disciplined for just cause. Whether an employee may be disciplined for leaving work without permission where no supervisor is available and the employee has requested that a co-worker advise a supervisor of the employee's absence will depend on the validity of the employee's reasons for leaving the workplace and past practice in the workplace.

Before disciplining an employee for leaving work without permission, the employer should ensure compliance with the leave provisions of the *Employment Standards Act, 2000*. First, the *Employment Standards Act, 2000* establishes various leave entitlements for employees: personal emergency leave, emergency leave, declared emergencies, reservist leave, family medical leave, and organ donor leave. The circumstances in which employees are entitled to take these leaves are reviewed below. The *Employment Standards Act, 2000* provides that an employee who wishes to take one of these leaves must advise the employer that he or she will be doing so. If advance notice is not possible, the *Employment Standards Act, 2000* requires the employee to advise the employer as soon as possible after beginning the leave. Therefore, while employers may normally expect some notice concerning these leaves (and should set out those expectations), the *Employment Standards Act, 2000* specifically contemplates situations in which the employee is not able to request such leave in advance. In these circumstances, the employee is required to advise his or her employer of the leave as soon as possible after its commencement. These provisions seem to contemplate urgent situations in which it is either impractical or impossible for the employee to advise his or her employer prior to commencing the leave. The *Employment Standards Act, 2000* prohibits an employer from disciplining or otherwise penalizing an employee for exercising a right under the *Employment Standards Act, 2000.* Accordingly, discipline imposed for failing to advise the employer in advance of a protected leave where it was not possible to do so and the employee advised the employer as soon as possible after commencing the leave is unlikely to be upheld.

a) — Personal Emergency Leave

The *Employment Standards Act, 2000* entitles employees who work for employers regularly employing 50 or more employees to ten days per year of unpaid job protected personal emergency leave. Personal emergency leave is to be provided in the following three situations:

- a personal illness, injury or medical emergency;
- the death, illness, injury or medical emergency of a family member; and
- an urgent matter that concerns a family member.

For the purposes of personal emergency leave, an employee's family members are deemed to include:

- the employee's spouse;
- a parent, step-parent, or foster parent of the employee, or the employee's spouse;
- a child, step-child, or foster child of the employee, or the employee's spouse;
- a grandparent, step-grandparent, grandchild, or step-grandchild of the employee, or the employee's spouse;

- the spouse of a child of the employee;
- the employee's brother or sister; and
- a relative of the employee who is dependent on the employee for care or assistance.

b) — Emergency Leave, Declared Emergencies

The *Employment Standards Act, 2000* gives employees the right to a leave of absence where an employee is unable to perform the duties of his or her position because of an emergency declared by the Lieutenant Governor in Council or the Premier and because one of the following criteria applies:

1. An order that applies to the employee is made under section 7.0.2 of the *Emergency Management and Civil Protection Act.* Section 7.0.2 of the *Emergency Management and Civil Protection Act* authorizes the Lieutenant Governor in Council, in certain circumstances, and with certain limitations, to make orders believed to be necessary and essential to prevent, reduce, or mitigate serious harm to persons or substantial damage to property. For example, the Lieutenant Governor in Council may make an order regulating or prohibiting travel or movement to, from or within a specified area.
2. An order that applies to the employee is made under the *Health Protection and Promotion Act.* The *Health Protection and Promotion Act* contains provisions that allow a medical officer of health, in certain circumstances, to order individuals to refrain from taking any action specified in the order.
3. The employee is needed to provide care or assistance to a specified family member. The specified family members are the same as those identified above for the purposes of personal emergency leave.

While other reasons may be prescribed, there are no prescribed reasons at this time.

It should be noted that the threshold criterion for emergency leave is that an emergency has been declared under section 7.0.1 of the *Emergency Management and Civil Protection Act* and the employee is, as a result, unable to perform his or her duties. There must be a causal connection between the employee not performing his or her duties and the declared emergency.

c) — Reservist Leave

The *Employment Standards Act, 2000* entitles an employee to a leave of absence without pay if the employee is a reservist and will not be performing his or her duties because the employee is deployed to a Canadian Forces operation outside of Canada, the employee is deployed to a Canadian Forces operation inside Canada that is or will be providing assistance in dealing with an emergency or its aftermath, or prescribed circumstances apply. At the time of writing, there are no prescribed circumstances that apply.

d) — Family Medical Leave

An employee is entitled to a leave of absence without pay of up to eight (8) weeks to provide care or support to a specified family member if a qualified health practitioner issues a certificate stating that the family member has a serious medical condition with a significant risk of death occurring within a period of 26 weeks or such shorter period as may be prescribed. The specified family members are:

- the employee's spouse;
- a parent, step-parent or foster parent of the employee;
- a child, step-child or foster child of the employee or the employee's spouse;
- a brother, step-brother, sister or step-sister of the employee;
- a grandparent or step-grandparent of the employee or employee's spouse;
- a grandchild or step-grandchild of the employee or the employee's spouse;
- a father-in-law, mother-in-law, step-father-in-law or step-mother-in-law of the employee;
- a brother-in-law, sister-in-law, step-brother-in-law or step-sister-in-law of the employee;
- a son-in-law or daughter-in-law of the employee or the employee's spouse;
- an uncle or aunt of the employee or the employee's spouse;
- the nephew or niece of the employee or the employee's spouse;
- the spouse of the employee's grandchild, uncle, aunt, nephew or niece;

- a foster parent of the employee's spouse; and
- a person who considers the employee to be like family member.

e) — Organ Donor Leave

The *Employment Standards Act, 2000* entitles an employee who undergoes surgery for the purpose of organ donation to a leave of absence without pay of up to 13 weeks (or for the prescribed period if applicable). Currently, there is no prescribed duration for organ donor leave so the 13 week maximum applies for all employees. To qualify, the employee must have been employed by his or her employer for at least 13 weeks. The employer may require the employee to provide a certificate issued by a legally qualified medical practitioner confirming that the employee has undergone or will undergo surgery for the purpose of organ donation. The leave may be extended if a legally qualified medical practitioner issues a certificate stating that the employee is not yet able to perform the duties of his or her position because of the organ donation and will not be able to do so for a specified period of time. While the leave may be extended more than once, the total extension period cannot exceed 13 weeks. Accordingly, the total maximum period of an organ donor leave is 26 weeks. An employee who wishes to take or extend an organ donor leave is required to give his or her employer at least two weeks of written notice unless the employee "must begin or extend the leave before advising the employer" in which case, the employee must advise the employer in writing as soon as possible after beginning or extending the leave.

4.3 — Lateness

An employee who fails to report for work in a punctual manner may be subject to discipline. However, an employer should not repeatedly ignore cases of lateness and then, without prior warning, discipline an employee for being late. The employer should seek an explanation from the late employee after each incident. If, on any occasion, the explanation establishes that the reasons for the lateness were clearly beyond the employee's control, the employer may decide that the employee should not be disciplined. However, a record should be made of the incident and the reasons why discipline was not imposed. An important consideration when assessing an employee's lateness is the amount of time by which the employee is late and the frequency with which the employee is late.

Generally, it is patterns of employee lateness or tardiness which will attract progressive discipline, rather than any single incident of lateness. Where a pattern of lateness emerges over some reasonable defined period of time (e.g. one to two months), progressive discipline will be issued at the end of each such block of time in which the incidents of lateness occur. However, even pattern lateness should not be the subject of discipline unless caused by factors within the employee's control.

4.4 — Dishonesty

Honesty is the touchstone of a viable employer-employee relationship. Any employee who is dishonest (e.g. who lies to his or her employer during an investigation, who misrepresents his or her qualifications, who obtains a secret commission or benefit, who wrongfully uses the employer's property, who falsifies company documents or who performs personal work on company time) puts his or her employment in jeopardy.

However, in all cases, the employer must carefully investigate the employee's conduct and must consider any and all extenuating circumstances before meting out discipline or discharging the employee.

For example, an employee who steals the employer's property or another employee's property may be subject to severe discipline, up to and including discharge. However, possession of another person's property will not necessarily constitute proof of theft and the employer should carry out a thorough investigation prior to making a final determination.

Mitigating factors may play a role. For example, if the theft was committed on the spur of the moment (as opposed to theft that is deliberate and planned) and the employee has a long service record without incident and apologizes immediately, an arbitrator may take the view that discharge is too severe. In such circumstances, the penalty may be reduced from a discharge to a lengthy suspension.

Similarly, the courts have held that dishonesty will only constitute just cause for discharge where it gives rise to a breakdown in the employment relationship. Not every case of dishonesty will justify a summary dismissal. In each case, a contextual analysis must be applied to determine whether the sanction imposed is proportional to the severity of the misconduct. To constitute just cause for dismissal, an employee must have engaged in deceitful conduct and the dishonesty must be of such a nature and degree to result in the breakdown of the employment relationship. Where the dishonesty occurs in the context of a relationship that requires a high level of honesty or trust because of the nature of the work, even a single incident may warrant dismissal, particularly if the employee's dishonesty violates an essential condition of the employment contract, breaches the faith inherent in the working relationship, or is fundamentally or directly inconsistent with the employee's obligations.

Significant Case Law

McKinley v. BC Tel (2001), 2001 CarswellBC 1336, 2001 CarswellBC 1335, [2001] 2 S.C.R. 161, 200 D.L.R. (4th) 385 (S.C.C.)

In *McKinley*, the Supreme Court of Canada clarified when an employee's dishonesty will warrant discharge without notice. The dishonesty must be proven on a balance of probabilities and its nature and degree must give rise to a breakdown of the employment relationship.

The Facts

During his sixteen-year career with BC Tel, Martin Richard McKinley held a variety of positions including controller, treasurer, and assistant secretary.

In 1993, McKinley, who was in his late forties, began experiencing high blood pressure as a result of hypertension. By June of 1994, McKinley's condition had worsened. On the advice of his physician, he took a leave of absence from work. McKinley then requested that he be returned to work in a position that carried less responsibility. BC Tel advised McKinley that it would attempt to find a suitable position for him. While at least two positions that McKinley was qualified for became available, he was not offered alternative employment. Rather, BC Tel terminated McKinley's employment. McKinley commenced a wrongful dismissal action claiming that BC Tel terminated his employment without just cause and without reasonable notice or pay in lieu thereof.

BC Tel took the position that McKinley's illness frustrated the employment contract and that BC Tel was therefore justified in treating the employment contract as being at an end.

At trial, the B.C. Supreme Court granted BC Tel leave to amend its pleadings to abandon the frustration defence and to argue instead that it had just cause to terminate McKinley's employment contract due to his dishonesty about his medical condition. BC Tel had learned that some time before McKinley's leave of absence, his physician had recommended a certain medication, beta-blockers, as the next step of treatment for his hypertension. McKinley did not disclose this information to BC Tel. By all accounts, this medication likely would have managed McKinley's hypertension with a minimum of side effects.

The trial judge decided that there was enough evidence to put the question of just cause before the jury. The trial judge told the jury that in order to find just cause, the jury must be satisfied that McKinley was dishonest and that the dishonesty was so egregious that it was "incompatible with the employment relationship". The jury found in favour of McKinley and awarded general damages, special damages, aggravated damages, and pension contributions.

On appeal, the B.C. Court of Appeal found that the trial judge had erred in instructing the jury that the employee's dishonesty would merit his discharge only if it was incompatible with the employment relationship. The Court of Appeal set aside the jury's verdict and ordered a new trial. McKinley appealed the Court of Appeal's decision to the Supreme Court of Canada.

The Decision

McKinley's appeal to the Supreme Court of Canada addressed the issue of whether dishonesty, in and of itself, could constitute just cause for dismissal.

The Court found that work is a fundamental aspect of an individual's life. Accordingly, any discipline should be proportional to the severity of the employee's misconduct. Applying this approach, the Court concluded that the appropriate test for determining whether dishonesty warrants dismissal for just cause is to consider whether the employee's dishonesty gives rise to a breakdown in the employment relationship.

The Court restored the trial judge's award with the exception of the award for aggravated damages, which was struck. The Court held that aggravated damages are only available where the employer's conduct is independently actionable. In other words, the employer's conduct must amount to a wrong that is separate from the breach of contract for failure to give reasonable notice of termination. The Court found that there was not enough evidence of an intention on the part of the employer to inflict mental distress on the employee to allow such an award.

The Implications

While dishonesty is always, of course, a serious workplace matter, it has many forms. Some forms of dishonesty, such as theft, will almost always warrant discharge. Other forms of dishonesty, such as withholding the truth, may not necessarily produce the same result. To justify discharge, the dishonesty must be proven on a balance of probabilities and must give rise to a breakdown of the employment relationship. Put differently, the question that must always be asked is whether there has been an irreparable breach of trust.

Significant Case Law

Dowling v. Ontario (Workplace Safety & Insurance Board) (2004), 246 D.L.R. (4th) 65, 2004 CarswellOnt 4923 (Ont. C.A.), leave to appeal refused (2005), 2005 CarswellOnt 2040, 2005 CarswellOnt 2039 (S.C.C.)

The Ontario Court of Appeal held that a senior employee, with long service and an exemplary performance record was nonetheless dismissed for just cause on the basis of dishonest and deceptive conduct that was inconsistent with his duties as a manager in a position of trust.

The Facts

Dowling was 50 years old, had 25 years of dedicated service with the Workplace Safety and Insurance Board ("WSIB") and was within a few months of early retirement. He was one of two managers in the WSIB's Ottawa office, supervising customer service employees who handled accounts of employers registered with the WSIB. Dowling had the discretion to authorize refunds of up to $25,000, and premium adjustments of up to $100,000. A few days prior to his dismissal, Dowling was commended by the WSIB for service "above and beyond".

Dowling developed a close personal relationship with an employer representative. He purchased two computers at a discount from one of the representative's clients. He also accepted $1,000 from the representative for authorizing a rate reclassification that resulted in a refund for one of her clients. Dowling was aware of the WSIB's code of conduct which prohibited employees from accepting direct or indirect benefits from any individual or organization external to the WSIB. When Dowling was confronted about these matters, he admitted receipt of the computers, but lied about the payment of money to him by the representative. Dowling and the employer representative also prepared a false receipt in an attempt to show that the $1,000 was a loan repayment. Upon discovering Dowling's misconduct, the WSIB terminated his employment for cause. Dowling sued for wrongful dismissal.

At trial, the judge found that Dowling's acceptance of the cheque for $1,000 may have given rise to considerations of conflict of interest. Nonetheless, the trial judge found that there was insufficient evidence that Dowling had used his position to gain a monetary benefit such that termination was justified. The trial judge concluded that Mr. Dowling had been wrongfully dismissed and awarded over $600,000 in damages against the WSIB, representing 24 months of pay. The WSIB appealed to the Court of Appeal.

The Decision

On appeal, the trial judge's decision was unanimously set aside and the action was dismissed. The Court of Appeal found that the trial judge had erred because he failed to apply the correct legal standard as set out by the Supreme Court of Canada in *McKinley v. BC Tel.* The Court of Appeal in *Dowling* found that the trial judge did not consider whether Mr. Dowling's misconduct gave rise to a breakdown in the employment relationship in all the circumstances of the case. Rather, he considered only the narrow issue of whether a single act of conflict of interest (accepting the $1,000) justified termination.

The trial judge also erred, according to the Court of Appeal, in interpreting the principle of proportionality established in *McKinley* as a "weighing" exercise, with the pattern of dishonesty at one end of the scale and Dowling's years of service at an exemplary level at the other end. The Court of Appeal held that the *McKinley* test does not involve a simple balancing of "good versus bad" employee conduct. Rather, it involves a determination of whether the full extent of the employee's misconduct, when considered within the surrounding facts and circumstances, gives rise to a breakdown in the employment relationship. This determination involves an assessment of the following:

1. The nature and extent of the misconduct;
2. The surrounding circumstances; and
3. Whether dismissal was warranted.

In considering the nature and extent of the misconduct, the Court of Appeal found that the trial judge failed to turn his mind to the following acts of misconduct:

- Dowling's purchase of computers at a discount from the employer representative's client, and his acceptance of the $1,000 constituted a conflict of interest;
- he lied to investigators during the initial interview by failing to disclose that he had received a cheque for $1,000 from an employer representative;
- he had continual contact with the employer's representative during the investigation;

- he repeatedly lied to the WSIB's Director of Human Resources Development during the second interview, claiming that the $1,000 was a repayment of a loan; and
- he prepared a false loan document in an attempt to conceal the money he received.

With respect to the surrounding circumstances, the Court of Appeal considered Dowling's age, long service, exemplary employment record and power and authority. The Court then balanced these considerations against the WSIB's code of conduct, Dowling's position of trust and the duty of honesty and impartiality he owed to the WSIB and the public.

Considering the foregoing, the Court of Appeal found that Dowling's misconduct was sufficiently serious to warrant dismissal on any of the following three basis: his dishonesty violated an essential term of the employment contract; it breached the faith inherent to the work relationship; and it was fundamentally inconsistent with his obligations to the WSIB.

The Court of Appeal summarized its findings as follows, at page 82:

> It was indispensable to the parties' employment relationship that Dowling exercise the powers of his position with honesty and impartiality, and exclusively in the interests of the WSIB and the public. The underpinnings of faith and confidence necessary to the parties' employment relationship were destroyed by Mr. Dowling's misconduct. When the various acts of misconduct are considered in the context of Mr. Dowling's position, the degree of trust reposed in him, and the public nature of the WSIB's responsibility, it is clear that summary dismissal was a proportionate response.
>
> [emphasis added]

The Court of Appeal concluded that Dowling's misconduct was so inconsistent with his duties that there was no basis on which the parties could continue in their employment relationship. Accordingly, Dowling's dishonesty was, in all the circumstances of the case, sufficiently serious to justify dismissal for cause.

The Implications

The Court rejected the notion that a long and otherwise exemplary record of service will in most cases outweigh serious misconduct. *Dowling* should not, however, be interpreted as standing for the proposition that any serious conflict of interest or incident of dishonesty will necessarily amount to cause for dismissal. In many cases, the cause standard will not be met on the basis of one incident of misconduct. At most, the decision in *Dowling* affirms the Supreme Court of Canada's view that misconduct cases, particularly those involving employee dishonesty, must be determined using a contextual approach. It is only through a careful analysis of all the relevant facts and circumstances of the case that the court can determine whether the misconduct in question amounts to a breakdown in the employment relationship, such that dismissal for cause is warranted.

4.5 — Sabotage/Property Damage

Arbitrators and courts have consistently held that an employer has the right to either suspend or, more commonly, discharge an employee who wilfully destroys the employer's property — especially if it creates an unsafe or dangerous situation. In order to substantiate a dismissal, the employer must demonstrate that the damage was done wilfully. Proof of wilfulness may be in the form of an admission by the employee involved or may be inferred from the circumstances. Where the damage was done while the employee was in a fit of rage or after the employee was provoked by a manager or another employee, the penalty of discharge must be carefully evaluated in light of any valid mitigating circumstances. However, serve discipline would still be properly imposed even if such circumstances exist.

4.6 — Fighting/Violence in the Workplace

Workplace violence is a challenging issue for human resources practitioners.

On September 17, 2008, the Ministry of Labour issued a consultation paper on workplace violence prevention. The consultation paper indicated that workplace violence is a growing concern. The paper cited a 2004 Statistics Canada survey "Criminal Victimization in the Workplace." According to this survey, 17 percent of violent victimization incidents in Canada occur at the workplace and this represents approximately 356,000 workplace violence incidents in a 12-month period across Canada. In 33 percent of workplace violence incidents, the victim worked in either healthcare or social assistance services, 14 percent of the workplace incidents involved victims in accommodation or food services, and 11 percent involved victims working in the education field.

Even if only a small percentage of the 356,000 annual workplace incidents results in a serious injury or death, this is nonetheless a staggering number. The consultation paper also noted the higher risk of violence in particular sectors as well as the increased risk of violence associated with certain types of work such as handling cash, protecting and securing valuables, transporting people and goods, and with certain work features such as a mobile workplace, public or community contact, working with unstable or volatile people, working alone or with just a few people, and working late nights or early mornings.

Against this background, the Ministry of Labour sought public input on whether the *Occupational Health and Safety Act* and its Regulations should be clarified or enhanced to further prevent and address workplace violence. As the consultation paper noted, under current *Occupational Health and Safety Act* provisions, employers must take every precaution reasonable in the circumstances for the protection of workers. This requirement has been in place for many years and is broad enough to require employers to take reasonable precautions to protect workers from workplace violence. However, the consultation paper expressly stated the government's expectation that employers protect their workers from violence at the workplace and indicated that Ministry of Labour inspectors proactively check for procedures to deal with workplace violence in workplaces with a higher risk of this occurring. The consultation paper specifically sought input as to whether the *Occupational Health and Safety Act* should be enhanced and clarified in relation to:

- definition of workplace violence;
- workplace violence prevention requirements;
- sector-specific requirements;
- domestic violence in the workplace; and
- work refusals.

A number of stakeholders submitted comments in response to the consultation and on April 20, 2009, the government announced it was introducing new legislation, Bill 168, to "tackle" workplace violence.

If the Bill is passed, the *Occupational Health and Safety Act* will be amended to impose various requirements with respect to workplace violence. Some of the key proposed changes include the following requirements:

1. Preparation of Policies with respect to Workplace Violence and Workplace Harassment — Under the Bill, employers would be required to prepare written policies with respect to (a) workplace violence and (b) workplace harassment.

2. Risk of Violence Assessment — Under the Bill, employers would be expressly required to carry out an assessment of the risk of workplace violence that may arise from the nature of the workplace, the type of work or the conditions of work. Employers would be required to advise the joint health and safety committee or representative of the results of the assessment and provide a copy of the assessment. If there is no joint health and safety committee or health and safety representative, the employer would be required to advise the workers of the results of the assessment and, if the assessment is in writing, provide copies on request or advise the workers how to obtain copies. Employers would be required to reassess the risk of violence "as often as is necessary" to ensure that the workplace violence policy and the workplace violence program (discussed below) continue to protect workers from workplace violence.

3. Employers must Develop and Maintain a Workplace Violence Program — Under the Bill, employers would be required to develop and maintain a program to implement the workplace violence policy. Required elements of the program would include: measures and procedures to control the risks identified in the workplace violence assessment; measures and procedures for summoning immediate assistance when workplace violence occurs or is likely to occur or when a threat of workplace violence is made; measures and procedures for workers to report incidents or threats of workplace violence to the employer or supervisor; and procedures governing how the employer will investigate and deal with incidents, complaints or threats of workplace violence. Additional elements may be prescribed by regulation.

4. Employer Obligations with respect to Domestic Violence — Under the Bill, employers would be specifically required to take every precaution reasonable in the circumstances for the protection of the worker if an employer becomes aware, or ought reasonably to be aware, that domestic violence that would likely expose a worker to physical injury may occur in the workplace.

5. Employers required to Provide Instruction and Information on the Workplace Violence Policy and Program — Employers will be required under the proposed legislation to provide appropriate information and instruction for workers on the contents of the

workplace violence policy and program along with any other information or instruction prescribed by regulation. Although currently an inspector can order an employer to provide training to employees on violence prevention, the proposed legislation will subject employers generally to these requirements, and specific training requirements may be prescribed by Regulation.

6. Employers will be required to Develop and Maintain a Workplace Harassment Program and to provide appropriate training.

7. New Work Refusal Procedures — The provisions of the *Occupational Health and Safety Act* dealing with work refusals would be amended under the proposed legislation to add workplace violence likely to endanger a worker to the list of circumstances under which a worker may refuse to work.

At the time of writing, Bill 168 has only recently been introduced, and the final form of the legislation remains to be seen. However, it is clear that protecting workers from workplace violence and harassment is a significant priority of the Ontario government and the Ministry of Labour in particular.

The cost of workplace violence is high. In addition to impacting the health and welfare of employees, violence and threats of violence result in loss of work, reduced efficiency, damage to an employer's reputation, increased insurance costs, and costs associated with improving security in the workplace. It is, therefore, vital for employers to have appropriate disciplinary mechanisms in place to address this health and safety issue.

Physically assaulting or even threatening to assault a manager, supervisor or fellow employee will generally attract the imposition of severe discipline. Not surprisingly, arbitrators view assaults upon managers and supervisors to be a challenge to the employer's authority and, therefore, more serious than an assault or a fight between two employees. However, the employee's state of mind of at the time of the incident is a significant consideration in determining the appropriate disciplinary penalty. Therefore, in both unionized and non-unionized workplaces, employers should consider whether the incident amounted to a momentary flare-up or was premeditated, whether the assault was provoked, and whether the employee apologized for the assault. It is also important to review the nature of the assault itself.

Was a weapon (or tool) used? Were there blows to the head or vital parts of the body?

Significant Case Law

Hammant Manufacturing Inc. v. United Steelworkers of Canada, Local 16506 (January 26, 2001), M.L. Tims, Arbitrator, [2001] O.L.A.A. No. 61 (Ont. Arb. Bd.)

In *Hammant*, the Arbitrator upheld the discharge of an employee for violence in the workplace. The Arbitrator found that the fact that the employee was allowed to return to work after engaging in threatening conduct did not amount to condonation as the parties had agreed to a "stay of proceedings".

The Facts

Keith Lynch, a welder with six and a half years of service, was dismissed from his employment on September 21, 2000.

The events leading up to the dismissal commenced on September 14th when Lynch swore at his supervisor several times. The next morning, the supervisor observed Lynch violently hammering a worktable while glaring at him. That afternoon, the supervisor again observed Lynch engaging in violent conduct. Specifically, Lynch was hitting the side of a container with a slag chipper, a heavy metal tool. Upon being confronted by the supervisor, Lynch approached him while tossing the tool in the air. Lynch moved closer and closer towards the supervisor and finally lunged at him with the slag chipper, stopping only a few inches away from the supervisor's face. Lynch denied that these events occurred and claimed that the supervisor was picking on him.

Later that day, the supervisor consulted with the company president. The president decided that the company would dismiss Lynch and that they would finalize the documentation on the next workday, which was Monday, September 18th. Lynch called in sick on Monday. That day, the union representative phoned the president. In the course of their discussions, the president advised the union representative that the company had "issues to deal with" relating to Lynch. The union representative suggested that they meet on September 21st to discuss the matter with Lynch. The president agreed to the meeting time as long as "the parties were prepared to 'stay the proceedings' ... planned until Thursday". The union representative agreed to this caveat. Lynch returned to work on September 19th, and worked until September 21st, when the meeting between the parties was held. Lynch was dismissed at that meeting.

The Decision

The Arbitrator found the evidence of the supervisor and the president to be credible. Although the supervisor was not injured in the incident, the Arbitrator found that Lynch's conduct was severe enough to warrant dismissal. In reaching that conclusion, the Arbitrator considered Lynch's prior disciplinary record (which included two suspensions and one written warning), Lynch's use of a weapon, and the lack of an apology or admission of wrongdoing by Lynch. The Arbitrator also noted that there was no provocation and that Lynch's conduct could not be viewed as a momentary flare-up.

The Arbitrator then dealt with the fact that while the incidents took place on September 15th, Lynch was allowed to return to work and was not dismissed until September 21st. The Arbitrator considered this evidence "troubling". The evidence, however, did not amount to condonation of Lynch's behaviour. First, the president permitted the arrangement resolving that he would "keep an eye" on Lynch. Second, the parties expressly agreed that while the company "had issues" to deal with, there would be a "stay of proceedings".

The Implications

The *Hammant* case is an example of discipline for workplace violence. It is significant as discharge was upheld notwithstanding that the supervisor was not injured. In fact, the employee did not physically assault the supervisor. Rather, the employee engaged in threatening behaviour. The *Hammant* case is also significant as it considers the effect of a delay in imposing discipline. As a general rule, allegations of misconduct in the workplace should be dealt as soon as possible and the employee should not be allowed to return to work until the matter has been resolved. A delay in the process can be interpreted as condonation of the conduct by the employer. If, however, it is not possible to resolve the issue immediately, the *Hammant* award provides a guidebook for handling the delay. To begin with, it is important for the employer to show that it is ready to act. With that in mind, should the union propose a delay in the procedure, it may be acceptable for the employer to allow the employee back to work. However, the employer should obtain the union's express agreement that the delay in implementing the discipline or holding the meeting is without prejudice to the employer's right to discipline the employee. The employer should also advise the union that it considers the matter to be serious. When the employee returns to work, he or she should be monitored carefully. It is important to note, however, that the Arbitrator in *Hammant* considered the circumstances in the case to be somewhat "unique". The delay was very brief and there was an explicit agreement with the union to "stay" the proceedings.

4.7 — Insubordination

An employee must follow a reasonable order issued by his or her employer. Failure to follow such an order will constitute insubordination and may be the subject of discipline. In order to justify discipline for insubordination, the employer must prove that an order was given, the order was clearly communicated to the employee, an individual with proper managerial authority gave the order, and the employee actually refused to comply with the order. The employer's case for insubordination is made stronger if the employee refuses even after being advised that disciplinary action will follow.

In a unionized environment, where an employee objects to an order given by a manager or supervisor, the employee generally must comply with the order and may later file a grievance. This is known as the "obey now — grieve later" principle. There are exceptions to the general principle. Where those exceptions apply, an employee should not be disciplined for insubordination. The following circumstances have been recognized as exceptions to the "obey now — grieve later" principle:

- where the order given would require the employee to perform an illegal act;
- where the employee concerned is a union official and the order would result in irreparable harm to the ability of the union representative to properly represent his or her members; and
- where an employee has a reasonable fear for his or her own health or safety or the health and safety of others.

In each of these circumstances, arbitrators have found that the potential harm from obeying the order outweighs the employer's interest in undisrupted production. Notably, an employee invoking one of these exceptions bears the onus of proving that it applies. The employee must also explain his or her basis for refusing the order to the supervisor.

4.8 — Sexual and Discriminatory Harassment

Sexual harassment in the workplace is expressly prohibited by the *Human Rights Code*. Workplace sexual harassment can be broadly defined as unwelcome conduct of a sexual nature or the creation of a poisoned work environment due to improperly "sexualizing" the workplace. Sexual harassment encompasses a wide variety of behaviours that merit discipline of varying degrees. Conduct that may constitute sexual harassment ranges from explicit posters or photographs displayed in the workplace to persistent propositions and unsolicited physical contact.

Accusations of sexual harassment are very serious. Such allegations must be investigated and handled with extreme care. An employer should avoid acting on false accusations. At the same time, an employer's failure to properly address well-founded accusations can, apart from giving rise to breaches of the *Human Rights Code*, cause adverse emotional and even physical effects to the victim of the harassment.

The law in this area is extremely complex. However, to justify discipline, an employer should be able to demonstrate that the offending employee knew, or ought reasonably to have known (based on the appropriate objective standard) that the conduct in question was unwelcome. To justify more severe forms of discipline, including discharge, an employer may be required to demonstrate that the offending employee engaged in a pattern of harassing behaviour, rather than in a single isolated act. A single very serious act of harassment, however, may be sufficient to immediately justify a severe disciplinary response. Other forms of harassment contrary to human rights legislation (e.g. racial or age harassment) are less common, but should also attract an appropriate disciplinary response, up to discharge in the most serious cases.

Significant Case Law

Simpson v. Consumers' Assn. of Canada (2001), 209 D.L.R. (4th) 214, 2001 CarswellOnt 4448 (Ont. C.A.), leave to appeal refused (2002), 2002 CarswellOnt 2654, 2002 CarswellOnt 2653 (S.C.C.)

In *Simpson*, the Ontario Court of Appeal found that after-hours conduct constituted sexual harassment, notwithstanding that it occurred outside the workplace.

The Facts

David Simpson was the executive director of Consumers' Association of Canada (the "Association"). After his employment was terminated for sexual harassment, Simpson sued the Association for wrongful dismissal.

The Ontario Court (General Division) agreed with Simpson that the Association did not have just cause to terminate his employment, finding that all of the alleged incidents of sexual harassment were either consensual or occurred outside of the workplace. The Court awarded Simpson 12 months pay in lieu of notice and an additional six months notice for the employer's bad faith conduct. The Association appealed the decision to the Court of Appeal.

The Decision

The Court of Appeal found that the lower Court erred by excusing the incidents as being outside the workplace, consensual or forgiven. The Court of Appeal concluded that cause for termination arose out of the following six incidents.

- Simpson initiated a sexually suggestive conversation with his 22-year old secretary, indicating to her that she would progress in the organization if she became sexually intimate with him. When she refused his advances, Simpson allowed their work relationship to deteriorate to the point where she felt she had to resign.
- Simpson carried on sexual conversations with the Association's legal counsel and took her to a strip club.
- Simpson had an affair with a secretary, the result of which was that the secretary received advantages over another secretary with whom Simpson was not involved. When the secretary ultimately terminated the relationship, their work relationship deteriorated to the point where she felt she had to resign.
- Simpson swam nude in the lake at his cottage in front of employees who had gone to the cottage to discuss business.

- Simpson got into a hot tub nude with a partially dressed secretary and other employees at a hotel following a board meeting.
- Simpson squeezed the buttocks of the Association's bookkeeper while she was bending over.

The Court of Appeal concluded that, for the purpose of analyzing the incidents in question, the "workplace" must be defined to include places other than the physical workplace. Rather, the workplace must include after-work interaction and places at which the employer sponsored events.

In part, the Court of Appeal's findings turned on the fact that Simpson was the employer's executive director. For example, the Court found that he could not hide behind the employer's lack of a sexual harassment policy, since such a policy would have been Simpson's responsibility to create. The Court also found that Simpson could not rely on the general acceptance in the workplace of sexual conversations and nudity because those elements only became part of the workplace when he introduced them.

The Implications

Conduct outside the physical workplace may constitute sexual harassment, particularly where a manager or supervisor is essentially "in control".

4.9 — Conflict of Interest

An employee owes a duty of fidelity and loyalty to his or her employer. Operating or participating significantly in a business that competes with the employer's business may violate that duty. Discipline may be appropriate where an employee engages in such a conflict of interest with the employer. Where direct competition is established, the employer will not be required to establish actual losses arising from the competition. The employer will only have to establish that there is a likelihood or the potential for such losses. A conflict of interest will not necessarily arise, however, where the conduct that the employee is engaged in does not directly compete with or detrimentally affect the employer's business.

4.10 — Off-Duty Conduct and Criminal Convictions

What an employee does on his or her own time is generally deemed to be his or her own business. However, an employer may discipline an employee for off-duty conduct where one or more of the following criteria are met:

- the employee's conduct harms the reputation of the employer's business;
- the employee's behaviour renders the employee unable to properly perform his or her duties;
- the employee's behaviour leads to the reasonable refusal or reluctance of other employees to work with him or her; and
- the employee's behaviour makes it difficult for the employer to direct the work of other employees or otherwise interferes with the efficient management of the employer's business.

Significant Case Law

***Peel Board of Education v. O.S.S.T.F.*, (sub nom. *Peel Board of Education v. Ontario Secondary School Teachers' Federation)* (2002), 105 L.A.C. (4th) 15, 2002 CarswellOnt 2430 (Ont. Arb. Bd.), additional reasons at (2001), 2001 CarswellOnt 5117 (Ont. Arb. Bd.)**

In *Peel Board of Education*, the Arbitration Board found that publicly airing racist and discriminatory beliefs while off-duty breached the employer's multiculturalism policy and justified discharge. Even though the discharge infringed upon the grievor's rights to freedom of expression and association under the *Charter of Rights and Freedoms* (the "*Charter*"), the discharge was demonstrably justified in a free and democratic society.

The Facts

Paul Fromm participated in conferences and meetings sponsored by individuals and organizations that openly supported white supremacist and anti-Semitic views. As a result, Fromm was discharged from his employment as a teacher after 23 years of service. The incidents leading up to the Fromm's discharge occurred entirely outside of the workplace. There was no evidence that Fromm ever made his views known in the classroom. The school board, having previously transferred Fromm for publicly uttering racist statements, treated the off-duty misconduct as a culminating incident. Fromm's discharge letter provided that he had persisted in breaching the school board's multiculturalism policy, despite being strongly warned in the past. The union filed a grievance, alleging that the discharge was without cause and that it violated Fromm's rights under the *Charter* (which applied to the employees because it was a public school board).

The Decision

The Arbitration Board reviewed extensive evidence and testimony that Fromm was an active advocate for white supremacy and racial discrimination. In particular, the Arbitration Board noted that Fromm's participation as a speaker at various conferences, rallies, and meetings made his racist and anti-Semitic views widely known in the community. The Arbitration Board found that these views, when espoused by a teacher who is entrusted with the duty to promote respect for human rights and ethnocultural equity, have a profound and damaging effect on students, staff, and the surrounding community. The Arbitration Board found that Fromm's activities contributed to a poisoned environment in the school system and represented a clear breach of the school board's policy on equality and multiculturalism. The Arbitration Board concluded that there was just cause for Fromm's discharge.

In addressing the alleged *Charter* violation, the Arbitration Board found that Fromm's freedoms of expression and association had likely been violated. The Arbitration Board then considered whether the violation was permitted by section 1 of the *Charter*. Section 1 of the *Charter* provides that the rights and freedoms protected by the *Charter* are subject "to such reasonable limits prescribed by law as can be demonstrably justified in a free and democratic society". Generally, for an impairment of a freedom to be saved by section 1, it must have a substantial and pressing purpose, the impairment must be rationally connected to that purpose, and the freedom must be minimally impaired. The Arbitration Board found that the standards embraced by the school board's multiculturalism policy constituted a pressing, substantial and worthwhile objective and that Fromm's discharge was rationally connected to that objective. The Arbitration Board further found that, given the destructive impact of Fromm's off-duty conduct and the fact that he had been warned in the past, discharge was justified. A lesser penalty, in the Arbitration Board's view, would not have remedied the very serious harm caused by Fromm's conduct. The fact that Fromm had previously been warned weighed heavily in support of the discharge. Accordingly, the Arbitration Board concluded that the discharge was demonstrably justified in a free and democratic society and should be upheld.

The Implications

Off-duty conduct by a teacher clearly can have adverse employment-related consequences. It is now clear that school boards' multiculturalism policies, which are designed to foster an environment of tolerance and equality, require a high standard of conduct by teachers, even when off-duty. In upholding Fromm's discharge, the Arbitration Board signalled that racist beliefs that are openly held and acted upon can create a poisoned environment and offend multiculturalism policies. It appears well settled now that the *Charter* protections available to individuals holding and acting on racist and intolerant beliefs will be very limited.

Where an employee's off-duty conduct is of a criminal nature, the specific factors that the employer should consider are:

- the nature of the employer's business;
- the type of criminal activities involved; and
- the duties and responsibilities of the employee.

An arbitrator or court will consider whether, in all the circumstances, there is a sufficient nexus between these three elements to justify discharge or whether the employer is simply acting out of an excessive and unjustified concern for public image and reputation.

Employers are generally required to establish criminal behaviour with "clear, cogent and convincing" evidence. A criminal conviction will typically be sufficient to prove the misconduct giving rise to the conviction. The only circumstances in which an employer should not rely on a criminal conviction as conclusive proof of the misconduct are where: (1) the criminal proceedings were tainted by fraud or dishonesty; (2) new evidence that was unavailable at the criminal trial conclusively undermines the criminal finding of guilt; or (3) it would be unfair to rely on the criminal proceedings. These are very limited circumstances. However, before an employer relies on a criminal conviction, it should provide the employee with an opportunity to advance any arguments as to why the criminal conviction should not be relied upon as conclusive proof of his/her misconduct.

A criminal acquittal does not preclude discipline or discharge. An acquittal simply means that the conduct was not proven beyond a reasonable doubt. In employment matters and arbitral proceedings, there is a lesser standard of proof: proof on a balance of probabilities. Accordingly, discipline may be appropriate even where an employee is acquitted if there is clear evidence of wrongdoing on a balance of probabilities standard.

Significant Case Law

Toronto (City) v. C.U.P.E., Local 79 (2003), 2003 CarswellOnt 4329, 2003 CarswellOnt 4328, [2003] 3 S.C.R. 77, 232 D.L.R. (4th) 385 (S.C.C.)

In *Toronto (City)*, the Supreme Court of Canada held that an Arbitrator erred in permitting a union to re-litigate an employee's criminal conviction. The Court found that the employee's conviction established that he had sexually assaulted the complainant.

The Facts

Glenn Oliver worked as a recreation instructor, leading various programs for children and mentally disabled adults at a recreation centre operated by the City. Oliver was convicted of sexually assaulting a minor who participated in the City's programs. At the criminal trial, the judge found that the issue was one of credibility and held that the minor was more credible than Oliver. Several days after the conviction, the City discharged Oliver. The City took the position that the conviction was evidence of a breach of trust and, given the City's responsibility to the public, was inconsistent with Oliver's continued employment.

At the subsequent arbitration hearing, the Arbitrator upheld Oliver's grievance and ruled that he had been dismissed without just cause. The Arbitrator found that the certificate of conviction and the transcript of evidence were *prima facie* evidence that Oliver had committed the acts of sexual assault. However, the Arbitrator found that it was open to him to determine the weight and probative value of those documents and it was open to the union to adduce evidence to rebut the certificate of conviction. The Arbitrator rejected the City's argument that it was an abuse of process to decide afresh whether Oliver committed the acts of assault for which he had been convicted. The Arbitrator concluded that Oliver was telling the truth and the minor was not. As a result, the Arbitrator reinstated Oliver with full compensation.

The Ontario Divisional Court quashed the Arbitrator's award along with two similar decisions rendered by the Ontario Government's Grievance Settlement Board. The Court forcefully recognized that a criminal conviction is the final word when it comes to an employee's guilt. The Court ruled that the union was not entitled to attack the "substance" of the certificate of conviction in order to "prove" that Oliver did not commit the offence of sexual assault as set out in the certificate of conviction.

The matter was then taken to the Court of Appeal. In a unanimous decision, the Court of Appeal upheld the Divisional Court's disposition of the case, but on the basis that public policy concerns precluded re-litigation. The Union appealed to the Supreme Court of Canada.

The Decision

The Supreme Court of Canada dismissed the appeal. The Court found that the facts of this case demonstrated a blatant abuse of process. The Court stated that the doctrine of abuse of process precludes parties from relitigating a dispute where to permit relitigation would bring the administration of justice into disrepute. The Court held that the union in this case was not entitled either at common law or under statute to challenge Oliver's conviction at arbitration. The Court concluded that in only the following very limited circumstances would the abuse of process doctrine cease to preclude relitigation in the context of a criminal conviction: (1) when the first proceeding is tainted by fraud or dishonesty; (2) when fresh, new evidence, previously unavailable, conclusively impeaches the original results; or (3) when fairness dictates that the original result should not be binding in the new context.

The Supreme Court of Canada concluded with this admonition to arbitrators: "[T]he arbitrator is considerably less well equipped than a judge presiding over a criminal court — or the jury — guided by rules of evidence that are sensitive to a fair search for the truth, an exacting standard of proof and expertise with the very questions in issue, to come to a correct disposition of the matter ... [In this case] the arbitrator was required as a matter of law to give full effect to the conviction".

The Implications

Based on the Supreme Court of Canada's reasoning, labour arbitrators should not allow the issue of criminal guilt to be re-litigated in the course of a challenge to disciplinary action unless the union can, at the very least, provide decisive new evidence or demonstrate a significant procedural flaw in the criminal proceeding.

As a general rule, therefore, employers can rely on a criminal conviction as proof that the employee committed the acts supporting the conviction.

In response to criminal charges, it may be permissible to suspend an employee without pay pending the outcome of criminal proceedings. The employee's interest in maintaining his or her livelihood must be balanced against the employer's interest in maintaining its reputation, productivity and morale. Arbitrators often apply the following principles in assessing the employer's response to off-duty criminal charges:

1. The off-duty conduct must present a reasonably serious and immediate risk to the employer's legitimate interests.

2. The onus is on the employer to satisfy the arbitrator of this risk. The employer must establish that the nature of the charge is potentially harmful to the employer's reputation, that it will render the employee unable to perform his or her duties, or that there is a risk to other employees or customers.

3. The employer must investigate the criminal charge to the best of its abilities before deciding on its response.

4. The employer must take reasonable steps to ascertain whether the risk of continued employment could be mitigated through closer supervision or a transfer to another position.

5. During a suspension, there is a continuing obligation on the employer to evaluate new information and consider reinstating the suspended employee to his or her position.

Applying these factors, employers should investigate criminal charges, and give the employee an opportunity to respond to the charges against him or her. In many cases, the opportunity for investigation will be limited as the employee may decline to participate in the employer's investigation prior to the criminal proceedings. After conducting an investigation, the employer should choose the option that protects its interests with the least interference in respect of the employee. Only where closer supervision or a transfer is not possible should a suspension without pay be considered. For example, depending upon the nature of the business, a suspension may be appropriate where an employee is charged with sexually assaulting a minor and his job is to work independently with young children.

4.11 — Breaching Company Rules

Employers typically promulgate company rules to regulate the workplace. Depending on the circumstances, an employee may be properly disciplined for breaching a company rule. Before disciplining an employee for breaching a company rule, an employer should ensure the following:

- the rule is consistent with the collective agreement or the employment contract;
- the rule is reasonable and promotes the employer's legitimate business interests;
- the rule is clear and unequivocal;
- the employee had notice of the rule;
- the employee had notice that breach of the rule could lead to discipline; and
- the employer has enforced the rule in a consistent manner.

4.12 — Absenteeism

a) — Innocent absenteeism

Innocent absenteeism occurs when an employee is absent from work due to illness, disability, or another legitimate health reason. Such health reasons may include alcoholism and drug dependency. Innocent absenteeism is distinguishable from culpable absenteeism, which occurs when an employee is absent from work for a non-legitimate reason. For example, the employee may oversleep or take an unapproved vacation day. Innocent absenteeism can be characterized by frequent short periods of absence or one or more extended periods of absence.

Discipline is not appropriate in cases of innocent absenteeism. If the employee's behaviour is blameless or faultless, the employer will *not* be justified in responding with disciplinary penalties.

Where an employee's absences, however, are so frequent and disruptive that the employee is no longer able to fulfill his or her side of the employment bargain, the employer may be justified in effecting a non-disciplinary dismissal. The employer must be able to establish that the employment relationship has been deprived of all viability. To establish this, the employer must be able to demonstrate the following:

- the employee has a past record of excessive absenteeism; and
- the employee is incapable of regular attendance in the future.

To establish a past record of excessive absenteeism, the employer must demonstrate that the employee's record is significantly worse than the workplace average over an extended period of time. Furthermore, the employee's absences must tangibly disrupt or impair the efficiency of the employer's business. The number of incidents of absenteeism is often more significant than the length of any particular absence as it is generally easier for an employer to accommodate one long absence as opposed to repeated and unpredictable absences.

Demonstrating that the employee is incapable of regular attendance in the foreseeable future is often difficult. At the very least, the employer should demonstrate that it is unlikely that the employee will be capable of maintaining an absenteeism record no worse than the average rate for a comparable group of employees. Proving future attendance can often be done by obtaining a medical certificate which addresses future prognosis or by the employer seeking to draw an adverse inference from the employee's past record of absenteeism.

Before dismissing an employee for innocent absenteeism, an employer must satisfy the following four procedural requirements.

- The employer must provide the employee with adequate warnings. Such warnings must indicate the employer's dissatisfaction with the employee's absenteeism. The employer should advise the employee that the business is detrimentally affected by the employee's absences and that an improvement is necessary. The warnings should be progressive in nature, building up to a warning that the employee's continued employment is in jeopardy. Finally, the warnings should be in writing and should clearly state that they are non-disciplinary.
- The employer must provide the employee with a sufficient opportunity to improve his or her attendance record to an acceptable standard.
- The employer must ensure that it deals with the problem of innocent absenteeism in a generally consistent manner.
- The employer must ensure that it has complied with all of its statutory duties, including, where applicable, its duty pursuant to the human rights legislation to accommodate an employee to the point of undue hardship. In Ontario, the employer must also ensure that it does not discipline an employee for taking a leave protected by the *Employment Standards Act, 2000* (e.g. a personal emergency leave.).

In a non-unionized environment, innocent absenteeism can also be cause for dismissal. From a legal perspective, such a dismissal is based on the common law doctrine of "frustration". If a court determines that the parties' employment contract has become frustrated or impossible to perform as a result of the employee's inability to work, the dismissal of the employee will be justified. To determine whether an employment contract has become frustrated, a court may consider the following factors:

- the applicable terms of the employment contract (if any) including sick leave provisions;
- the length of time the employment was likely to last, if not for the employee's illness or injury;
- the nature of the employment;
- the nature of the illness or injury, how long it has existed, and the prospects for recovery; and
- the period of past employment.

The above factors are interrelated and cumulative and may not necessarily be the only factors taken into account by a court.

Ultimately, the longer the employment relationship and the greater the indications of commitment and loyalty throughout the relationship (e.g. a long term disability plan), the more difficult it will be to establish that a contract of employment has been frustrated.

In both the unionized and the non-unionized context, where an employee's absences are caused by an underlying disability, a discharge for absenteeism could be challenged on the basis that the employer failed to accommodate the disabled employee up to the point of undue hardship. Accordingly, before any discharge for absenteeism is effected, the employer should review all relevant circumstances and ensure that it has fulfilled its statutory duty to accommodate disabled employees.

Significantly, the jurisprudence suggests even if an employer takes no steps to terminate the employment relationship, an employee may assert that his or her employment has been frustrated and that he or she is therefore entitled to statutory termination and severance pay pursuant to the *Employment Standards Act, 2000*. Interestingly, it is the Employment Standards Branch policy that this approach should not be followed and the employer must take some action (express or by implication) to terminate the employment relationship.

Significant Case Law

St. Joseph's General Hospital v. O.N.A. (2006), 148 L.A.C. (4th) 326, 2006 CarswellOnt 4899 (Ont. Arb. Bd.)

In *St. Joseph's*, a labour Arbitrator "deemed" that an employee's employment had effectively come to an end as a result of frustration of contract in circumstances where the employer had not taken any steps to terminate the employment relationship. The Arbitrator concluded that as the employment relationship had been frustrated, the employee was entitled to statutory severance pay pursuant to the *Employment Standards Act, 2000*.

The Facts

The grievor, Bridget Glynn, was a full-time registered nurse who suffered a workplace injury to her back in 2001. A brief attempt to return to work in 2002 was unsuccessful. While ONA and the Hospital canvassed modified work alternatives, no suitable accommodation was available. Glynn completed a labour market re-entry plan with the Workplace Safety and Insurance Board, but remained unable to work due to her injuries.

In 2004, ONA launched a grievance on behalf of Glynn, seeking a declaration that her employment with the Hospital had become frustrated. Arbitrator Luborsky, who heard the initial grievance, determined that ONA had not met the onus of establishing that Glynn was "incapable of fulfilling her employment obligations at the present time and into the foreseeable future." Accordingly, that grievance was dismissed. A second grievance was filed in 2005 and proceeded to arbitration before Arbitrator Randall.

Before Arbitrator Randall, ONA argued that given that the Hospital was unable to accommodate Glynn, by operation of law, her employment was frustrated and thus severed. As a result, Glynn was entitled to severance pay pursuant to the *Employment Standards Act, 2000*.

The Hospital argued that it had taken no positive action to dismiss Glynn. The Hospital asserted that the Arbitrator, therefore, had no authority to deem Glynn's employment terminated.

The Decision

Arbitrator Randall had no hesitation in finding that Glynn's condition was permanent and prevented her from performing any work for the Hospital in the foreseeable future. The Arbitrator also expressed doubt that a small hospital like St. Joseph's would ever be in a position to offer Glynn a position within her restrictions. The Arbitrator noted that the period of accommodation is not indefinite, particularly where the employee has no reasonable prospect of returning to work. In the circumstances, the Arbitrator determined that accommodation was exhausted.

The Arbitrator was then left with the question of whether a labour arbitrator has the requisite authority to declare an employment relationship to be "deemed terminated" due to frustration. Despite the Hospital's argument that the Arbitrator did not have jurisdiction to make such a declaration in the absence of a "deemed termination" provision in the collective agreement, Arbitrator Randall accepted the argument on behalf of ONA that authority could be found in the *Employment Standards Act, 2000*. Section 63(1) of the *Employment Standards Act, 2000* provides:

> 63. (1) An employer severs the employment of an employee if, (a) the employer dismisses the employee or otherwise refuses or is unable to continue employing the employee;

After quoting the provision, the Arbitrator stated at pages 333-334:

> Several things are noteworthy. The provision was amended in 2002, by adding the words in italics. The amendment clearly broadened the meaning to be given to "what constitutes severance". Formerly, a severance required one of two actions by the employer: dismissing the employee or refusing her employment. Now, finding an employer action is no longer a condition precedent to severance; severance also occurs when "the employer ... is unable to continue employing the employee". The inquiry under this arm of entitlement is simply whether an objective state of affairs exists.

Having found that Glynn's employment had become frustrated, the Arbitrator rejected the Hospital's argument that it needed to take some positive action in order to sever her employment.

Arbitrator Randall also rejected the Hospital's assertion that the employment relationship should not be deemed terminated because disabled employees continued to accrue seniority while off work on a WSIB disability claim, pursuant to the terms of the collective agreement. The Arbitrator instead found at pages 335-336:

> While the inference to be drawn from it is that the parties intend the employment relation to continue for some unstated duration, the provision cannot be read as occupying the entire field. It certainly does not trump the statute. It cannot prevent the Grievor from asserting that her employment has come to an end, that her seniority rights no longer have any value, and that she would like, therefore, to be paid her statutory minimum, and I so find. A contrary finding — that the Grievor must continue to live in a state of limbo, until the Employer acts — makes little sense. It raises issues of potential mischief in the statutory interpretation and may well breach the Employer's

duty, set out in article B-3 of the Local Agreement, to "exercise its rights and administer the Collective Agreement reasonably and fairly".

In the result, the Arbitrator found that Glynn's employment had become frustrated and that her employment was deemed terminated for purposes of the *Employment Standards Act, 2000.* Accordingly, Glynn was entitled to statutory severance pay.

The Implications

In 2005, the Ontario Court of Appeal decided that an exemption under the former *Employment Standards Act* that disentitled employees whose employment was frustrated by disability from receiving statutory severance pay was unconstitutional. As a result, the Ontario government amended Regulation 288/01 under the *Employment Standards Act, 2000* in October 2005. Not only was the exemption from severance pay for employees whose employment was frustrated by illness or injury eliminated, but the legislature also removed the equivalent exemption which applied to notice of termination or termination pay. Accordingly, as the law currently stands, an employee whose employment comes to an end as a result of frustration due to illness or injury is entitled to both termination and severance pay.

Given that frustration of contract due to illness or disability no longer precludes employees from claiming termination and severance pay under the *Employment Standards Act, 2000*, employers can anticipate that more and more employees will be seeking to receive their statutory entitlements, even when the employer has taken no action to sever the relationship. On the basis of the *St. Joseph's* decision, it is possible that adjudicators hearing such claims will "deem" their employment to be terminated, where sufficient evidence of frustration is advanced. However, the party alleging frustration of contract will still bear the onus of establishing that there is no reasonable prospect of the employee returning to work in the foreseeable future, even with accommodation.

b) — Culpable absenteeism

In contrast to innocent absenteeism, culpable absenteeism is a form of misconduct that warrants discipline, up to and including discharge, in appropriate circumstances. Culpable absenteeism includes unauthorized lateness, early departures, extended breaks and failure to call in.

The primary challenge in disciplining an employee for culpable absenteeism is establishing that the absence is indeed culpable. Unless the employer can establish that a particular absence is blameworthy, the employer must assume that the absence is innocent. Clear examples of culpable absenteeism include oversleeping, attending a sporting event, or taking an unapproved vacation day. However, the legitimacy of excuses such as "I got caught in a blizzard" and "public transportation was delayed" may be difficult to determine, especially if the employer has accepted such excuses in the past.

In some cases, inclement weather has been found to be a justifiable explanation for an absence suggesting that such absences should be treated as innocent. For example, in *Alexander and Treasury Board (Veterans' Affairs)*, [1987] CPSSRB No. 167 (R. Young), the Arbitrator considered whether discipline for failure to report to work was legitimate. The employee claimed that he did not report for work because he had been caught in a snow storm in the course of his return from a visit with his parents. The employee claimed he was forced to stop and stay overnight because the roads were impassable. During the grievance process, the employee submitted to the employer a letter from an individual confirming that the employee and his family spent the night at her home as the road was officially closed to all traffic. In addition, the employee submitted a letter from the sheriff's office confirming the road closure and that the "weather and road conditions were extremely hazardous due to blowing and drifting snow". In the circumstances, the Arbitrator concluded that while the employee did not have permission to be away from work, he was "unavoidably prevented from attending". The Arbitrator found that no discipline was appropriate stating that even though the absences were unauthorized they were "reasonable, understandable and verifiable".

While inclement weather may be a legitimate reason for being late or absent, each individual employee's circumstances should be thoroughly analyzed and employees questioned as to the reason for their absences before any conclusions are reached as to the legitimacy of each individual's absence. If other employees were able to attend work on time and were arriving from the same area, absent distinguishing circumstances, it may be reasonably argued that neither lateness nor absence is justifiable. In each case, it must be determined whether the employee took all reasonable steps to apprise the employer of the absence and whether the employee returned to or attended work as expeditiously as possible. While inclement weather may be sufficient to justify lateness in some cases, it may not be a legitimate explanation for an entire day's absence. Furthermore, the cases do not suggest that leaving early without permission is justified as a result of poor weather. At the very least, such excuses should be treated in a consistent manner.

Finally, in order to discharge an employee for culpable absenteeism, the employer must have instituted progressive disciplinary measures to warn the employee that his or her employment is in jeopardy.

Significant Case Law

Windsor (City) v. Canadian Union of Public Employees, Local 543 (Windsor Municipal Employees), [2002] O.L.A.A. No. 153 (Williamson)

In *Windsor (City)*, the Arbitrator found that a unilaterally imposed attendance management program was unreasonable. The Arbitrator found that the program contravened the collective agreement and the accommodation obligations under the Ontario *Human Rights Code*.

The Facts

The City unilaterally implemented an "Attendance at Work" policy involving the monitoring of sick leave occurrences over the course of a 12-month period.

Under the policy, any employee who exceeded four sick leave occurrences in a 12-month period was required to meet with his or her supervisor to review the attendance record, discuss the impact of lost time, and set a target for the next three-month period. If an employee failed to meet the objectives set at the meeting, a follow-up meeting would be held to re-address the issues and set new goals for improved attendance. If the meetings failed to improve the employee's attendance record, the City reserved the right to dismiss the employee for innocent absenteeism. The purpose of the program was not to be punitive but rather to ensure that all employees were "provided with the necessary guidance and encouragement to attend work on a regular basis". The union grieved the policy, arguing that it was disciplinary, unilaterally imposed, inconsistently applied, and contrary to the sick leave provision set out in the collective agreement.

The Decision

The Arbitrator found that the policy violated virtually all the accepted criteria for attendance policies. The Arbitrator rejected the City's contention that the policy was not disciplinary, noting that the policy was designed to correct unacceptable attendance behaviour. He also noted that if an employee's attendance did not improve after receiving several letters, the policy called for the employee to be referred for a medical examination, which could lead to the employee's dismissal. Despite the fact that an employee had yet to be dismissed under the policy, the Arbitrator found that it had clear punitive consequences and was properly regarded as a disciplinary policy.

The Arbitrator also found that the policy had not been consistently applied. For this reason alone, the Arbitrator held that the grievance should succeed.

The Arbitrator further noted that the policy failed to distinguish between culpable and non-culpable absences and made no provision for assessing an employee's individual circumstances or the particular reasons behind the absences. Instead, the program was based solely on the number of days an employee had been absent, which purportedly would give the employer just cause to dismiss an employee for culpable or non-culpable absenteeism. The Arbitrator noted that an employer may, in some cases, be able to dismiss an employee for non-culpable absenteeism, but only where it can be established that the employee has a record of undue absenteeism and is incapable of regular attendance in the future. The policy failed to establish either of those grounds.

Lastly, the Arbitrator pointed out that the ability to dismiss an employee for non-culpable absenteeism is strictly limited by the Ontario *Human Rights Code*, which requires accommodation of employees with disabilities to the point of undue hardship. The policy clearly disregarded the duty to accommodate.

The Arbitrator directed the City to withdraw the policy and expunge all letters and notations in employee files arising from its application.

The Implications

Attendance management programs must meet several requirements in order to be valid: they must be reasonable, clear, uniformly applied, consistent with the collective agreement, and in compliance with the accommodation obligations arising under human rights legislation. Although the issue is generally addressed on a case-by-case basis, it is almost certain that a policy will be struck down where it fails to meet these criteria. The *Windsor (City)* case adds to the body of case law on the issue and confirms that an employer cannot implement an attendance policy that imposes "discipline" for non-culpable absenteeism. Accordingly, any policy or program must clearly distinguish between culpable and non-culpable absences.

c) — Employment Standards Leaves

When assessing employees' absenteeism, employers should ensure that all applicable statutory requirements regarding leaves of absence are observed.

As set out earlier, the Ontario's *Employment Standards Act, 2000* provides certain employees with various unpaid job protected leaves. Employers must determine how those leave days will be treated for the purposes of an attendance management program.

In general, the prudent response is that leaves under the *Employment Standards Act, 2000* should not be included as "monitored" incidents under an attendance management program. However, if any leaves under the *Employment Standards Act, 2000* are to be included in an attendance management program, consideration should be given to the purpose of the leave. For example, if an employee takes leave for personal illness, injury or medical emergency, an employer may wish to include such days in the program since the absences are similar to sick days. However, if the purpose of the leave is bereavement or the illness, injury or medical emergency of a family member, such time off should likely not be considered for the attendance management system since absences for such things as bereavement are generally "non-monitored" absences.

4.13 — Performance Issues

Discipline may be imposed when an employee's work performance is unsatisfactory. Dismissal is not generally warranted, however, for a single incident of poor work performance. An alternative to applying the disciplinary process is to treat the poor performance as non-culpable and deal with it in the same manner as non-culpable absenteeism.

Establishing just cause for discharge based on unsatisfactory performance can be very difficult. To establish just cause for disciplining an employee for poor performance, an employer will generally be required to demonstrate the following:

- the employer has established objective and reasonable performance standards;
- the standards were clearly defined and were communicated to the employee;
- the employee received adequate training and instruction;

- the employee was specifically warned that he or she was not meeting the required standards and that his or her employment would be in jeopardy if he or she continued to fail to meet such standards;
- the employer afforded the employee a reasonable period of time in which to improve his or her performance; and
- the employee ultimately failed to achieve the standards.

The minimum performance standards must be as specific and detailed as possible. It is not sufficient to simply state, for example, "you are not performing at the minimum level of a data entry clerk". The performance standards must also be objective. For example, for a salesperson, an objective performance standard would be a requirement to make a certain number of cold calls or follow up calls per week. By way of contrast, a requirement to sell a certain amount of product each week may not be considered objective.

The amount of time that must be provided to an employee to improve his or her performance will depend upon the nature of the position and the deficiencies. As a general proposition, the more skilled the position, the more time that may be required for the employee to legitimately improve. On the other hand, in an unskilled position, a long period of time may not be necessary to provide the employee with a reasonable period to improve his or her performance.

The employer must document the employee's performance over time and may ultimately rely on the doctrine of the culminating incident to justify the discipline that is imposed. When the problem first arises, the employee should be told of any relevant standards or expectations with which he or she is expected to comply. At that time, the employee should be provided with copies of any relevant policies or rules. It is also useful to afford the employee an opportunity to discuss the reasons for the problem as well as possible solutions. Accurate notes of any meetings or discussions should be made. Employers may also issue a letter to the employee, which clearly details and confirms the employer's expectations, the employee's failure to meet those expectations, and the consequences of the employee failing to meet expectations in the future.

The following is an example of a letter that may be sent to an employee if verbal discussions do not result in improved performance.

Dear Mr. Doe:

Re: Unacceptable Job Performance

As you are aware, we have been very concerned with your ongoing work performance for some time now. These concerns have been brought to your attention verbally. Unfortunately, however, the situation has now reached the point where these concerns must be documented in writing.

The following are the minimum performance standards/expectations in your position:

> *[OUTLINE IN A SPECIFIC AND DETAILED MANNER ALL THE MINIMUM PERFORMANCE EXPECTATIONS OF THE POSITION]*

Your work performance is below the above outlined minimum performance standards/expectations. Specifically, your performance is below these minimum standards/expectations in the following areas:

> *[OUTLINE THE DEFICIENCIES]*

Your performance below the minimum required standards/expectations is not acceptable and cannot be tolerated. This letter constitutes a written warning that an improvement to the minimum standards is required, failing which your employment will be in jeopardy.

We will review this matter with you again on *[DATE]*, in order to determine if the necessary improvement has occurred. If we can help you in any way to improve your performance to these minimum standards/expectations, please speak to *[APPROPRIATE MANAGER OR SUPERVISOR]*.

We sincerely hope that your performance does improve in the future and that you can become a valued member of the workforce.

ABC Inc.

DATED ....

Signed .... Employee

For unionized employees, continued problems should be the subject of progressive disciplinary action. For non-unionized employees, a series of warnings are typically provided before a final warning letter is issued.

At the first review meeting, after the employee has been advised of his or her deficiencies, the employee may have improved in some but not all areas. In this situation, a follow-up letter should be issued identifying those areas where improvement has occurred, but again outlining the areas where improvement is still necessary. As long as the employee is moving towards the minimum performance standards, a discharge for just cause is unlikely to be upheld.

Finally, employers should ensure that employee evaluations or performance appraisals are honest and specific. Managers and supervisors often have a tendency to overlook performance problems in appraisals. Sometimes, they are simply unwilling to take the time required to accurately document performance problems. Other times, positive appraisals are used to encourage employees. Employers should ensure that all managers and supervisors are advised of the importance of accurately documenting employees' performance, including areas of deficiency and areas needing improvement. Caution should also be exercised in granting promotions to employees who are not performing up to standard as such actions may be inconsistent with later discipline for poor performance.

4.14 — Last Chance Agreements

An employer typically enters into a last chance agreement when it believes that the employee's conduct constitutes just cause for dismissal or the employee has been discharged and filed a grievance. Rather than discharge the employee or proceed with arbitration, the parties enter into a "Last Chance Agreement" (or "LCA"). The LCA allows the employee to maintain his or her position but under certain specified conditions. A LCA usually provides that a breach of any of its conditions constitutes cause for immediate dismissal.

Arbitrators are generally reluctant to interfere with the enforcement of a LCA. However, if the LCA does not expressly limit an arbitrator's jurisdiction to modify the penalty imposed, an arbitrator may consider mitigating factors and substitute a lesser penalty than that specified in the agreement. For example, an arbitrator may mitigate a penalty of discharge if there is doubt as to whether the employee understood the terms of the agreement or the employee is discharged for behaviour unrelated to the original agreement.

Even if the LCA limits the arbitrator's jurisdiction, the agreement may not be enforced if the conduct giving rise to the agreement relates to a prohibited ground of discrimination (e.g. disability under the *Human Rights Code*) and the employer has failed to fulfill its duty to accommodate. For example, where an employee's absences are known to be caused in part by a disability (e.g. alcoholism) and the parties enter into an agreement whereby the employee is required to meet a standard not required of other employees (e.g. perfect attendance), a discharge for breaching the agreement may constitute discrimination contrary to the *Human Rights Code*.

An employer can argue that an LCA is, in and of itself, a form of accommodation. Accordingly, the LCA should include a clause setting out the parties' agreement that the steps taken by the employer, including the execution of the LCA, amount to reasonable accommodation. The clause should provide that any further steps beyond the LCA would constitute undue hardship to the employer. However, the employer should not rely on such a clause alone. No matter how well drafted, an LCA, without further efforts to accommodate the employee, is unlikely to satisfy the employer's human rights obligations. The employer should be prepared to present evidence (of which the agreement is but one piece) establishing its efforts to accommodate the employee.

Employers should expect every aspect of a LCA to be scrutinized by the union, the affected employee and the arbitrator or court. Prudent employers will carefully draft any LCA to maximize the likelihood of the agreement being enforced. The agreement should be simple, clear and straightforward. An employer should consider the following terms when drafting a LCA:

- The employee should recognize the nature of his or her problem (e.g. that he or she suffers from alcoholism).
- Any steps the employer has taken to help the employee with his or her problem should be outlined in the agreement.
- The parties to the agreement may include a clause that outlines their agreement that the steps taken to help the employee with his or her problem fulfill their respective obligations of "accommodation" under the Ontario *Human Rights Code*.
- The conditions of continued employment should be specifically outlined and the employee should commit to meeting those conditions.
- The agreement should provide that any violation of its terms will result in the employee's discharge.
- The agreement should stipulate that any breach of its terms constitutes undue hardship for the employer.

- The agreement should state that if the employer elects not to invoke dismissal for a breach of the agreement, that forbearance will not be raised as any type of waiver or estoppel.
- In a unionized environment, the agreement should expressly limit the jurisdiction of an arbitrator to modify the penalty provided therein. Specifically, an arbitrator should not have the jurisdiction to substitute a lesser penalty for discharge once it has been determined that the terms of the agreement were breached.
- An expiry date should be specified in the agreement. Generally, the agreement should remain in effect for no more than one or two years.
- Both the employee and the union, if any, should be parties to and sign the agreement.

Significant Case Law

Cleaver Brooks v. U.S.W.A., Local 7257(January 17, 2000), W.B. Rayner, Arbitrator, [2000] O.L.A.A. No. 66 (Ont. Arb. Bd.)

In *Cleaver Brooks*, the Arbitrator upheld the discharge of an employee for excessive absenteeism (resulting from alcohol abuse) after the expiry of a last chance agreement.

The Facts

After the break up of his marriage, Chris Neil developed a serious drinking problem. As a result, he missed an unacceptable number of days of work and was eventually discharged. Neil subsequently told his employer that he had a drinking problem and needed help. Neil was reinstated pursuant to a last chance agreement with the employer and the union. The last chance agreement required Neil to maintain the plant attendance average for 12 months and to enrol in an approved counselling program. Failure to meet those conditions would result in Neil's discharge from employment. The agreement specified that the employer's actions constituted "accommodation" within the meaning of the *Human Rights Code*.

When Neil returned to work, he failed to meet the condition relating to his attendance. Giving Neil the benefit of the doubt, the employer did not invoke the agreement. However, upon the expiry of the agreement, Neil's attendance "went into a tailspin" and the employer discharged him. There was no dispute that Neil's absences resulted from alcohol abuse.

The Decision

The Arbitrator held that alcoholism is a handicap that requires accommodation. However, the Arbitrator recognized that alcoholism and its treatment involve a strong element of volition on the part of the victim. As such, the Arbitrator accepted the employer's argument that the duty to accommodate requires the employer to take the following steps:

- understand the nature of the problem;
- give the employee a reasonable amount of time to correct the problem; and
- take all reasonable steps to assist the employee in correcting the problem.

The Arbitrator found that the recognition in the last chance agreement that the employer's efforts constituted accommodation was not necessarily sufficient to satisfy the duty to accommodate. The Arbitrator considered whether the employer should have entered one more last chance agreement requiring Neil to seek more professional help. The Arbitrator noted that while Neil had technically complied with the agreement, he reverted to his problem behaviour shortly after the expiry of the agreement. As a result, the Arbitrator concluded that Neil's rehabilitative potential was low enough to relieve the employer of any further duty to accommodate. The grievance was, therefore, dismissed and the discharge upheld.

The Implications

Last chance agreements are appropriate in some circumstances. If carefully drafted and implemented as part of a comprehensive accommodation program, a last chance agreement may be a useful tool for dealing with an employee who has not responded to progressive discipline or other accommodation measures. The last chance agreement may cause the employee to recognize the severity of the problem and cause him or her to seek treatment. In the case of an employee suffering from alcoholism, for example, this may cause the employee to successfully complete a rehabilitation program. If the employee does not successfully rehabilitate himself or herself or the problem is not conducive to rehabilitation, a last chance agreement that is properly drafted and implemented may evidence the employer's attempts at accommodation. It is important to remember, however, that a last chance agreement is not a substitute for accommodation and will only be upheld if it is part of a comprehensive accommodation program designed to assist the employee in performing the essential duties of his or her job.

Chapter 5: Elements of the Disciplinary/Discharge Letter

5.1 — Introduction

Once an employer has decided to impose a particular disciplinary penalty, the next step is usually drafting the disciplinary letter. An employer should use clear and direct language. The letter should refer as much as possible to objective facts rather than subjective perceptions. After reading a disciplinary letter, the employee should know the exact source of the employer's concern as well as the improvements he or she is required to make. The employee should not have to "read between the lines" to understand the employer's message.

In any disciplinary letter, there are certain elements that should be present to ensure that the letter is effective and accomplishes the employer's purposes. These elements are described below.

5.2 — The Disciplinary Record

An employer should briefly review the relevant elements of the employee's disciplinary record. The letter should set out any relevant verbal warnings, written warnings, and suspensions.

5.3 — The Infraction

The disciplinary letter must include a description of the infraction, including a broad overview of the material facts. The employee and any other reader should be able to understand the reason for the discipline and the employer's expectations with respect to future conduct.

5.4 — The Disciplinary Penalty Being Applied

The disciplinary penalty being administered should be clearly set out. In the case of a disciplinary suspension, the length of the suspension as well as the dates upon which the suspension will begin and end should be identified.

5.5 — Available Employee Support / The Positive Aspect of the Disciplinary Penalty

Where appropriate, an employer should consider stressing the positive qualities that will enable the employee to correct the behaviour in question. The disciplinary letter should set out how to correct the behaviour and the tools available to assist the employee in that task. For example, the employee may be directed to an employee assistance program or advised of training opportunities. The importance of properly performed work and its significance to the success of the employer's business should also be stressed. Above all, the disciplinary measure should not be so coercive as to have an overly negative effect on the employee's self-esteem or morale. Such an effect would be counter-productive to the ultimate goals of the disciplinary measure.

5.6 — Serving Notice of Future Discipline

Once the verbal warning stage has been passed, every written warning should clearly state that the situation is increasing in severity. The employer should specifically warn the employee that if the behaviour is not corrected, the employer may take more severe disciplinary steps, up to and including discharge. By the suspension stage, at the latest, the employee should be put on notice that any further failure to correct his or her behaviour will lead to dismissal.

Such warnings demonstrate to the employee as well as to any arbitrator or court that the employee was given an opportunity to improve his or her behaviour before the employer progressed to more severe disciplinary penalties.

The following is a sample disciplinary letter dealing with the hypothetical situation of an employee who reported late for a scheduled shift. The letter incorporates the various elements set out above. However, every situation is different and the appropriate disciplinary response will depend upon an analysis of all relevant factors.

	Dear Ms Smith: *Re: Three-day suspension*
Reference to the disciplinary record	On February 1, you were given a verbal warning for reporting to work late. On February 14, you were given a written warning for reporting for work late on February 12 and 13. On March 1, you were suspended for one (1) day for reporting to work late on February 27 and 28.
Description of the infraction	On March 15, you reported for your scheduled shift approximately twenty-five (25) minutes late. On March 16, you reported for your scheduled shift approximately twenty (20) minutes late. You did not provide ABC Inc. with a legitimate justification for any of these incidents.
Available employee support	This misconduct is unacceptable to ABC Inc. ABC Inc. requires all of its employees to report to work in a timely manner. Your lateness interferes with the efficiency of ABC Inc.'s production processes. If your lateness is due to personal problems that you may be encountering, you may wish to contact ABC Inc.'s Employee Assistance Program.
The disciplinary penalty	Your misconduct leaves us with no choice but to impose a three (3) day suspension without pay from March 18 to March 20 inclusive. You will report to work on March 21. We trust that this discipline will encourage you to correct your behaviour in the future so that you may become a satisfactory employee.
Notice	Please be aware that if you engage in further misconduct of any kind, you may be subject to more severe discipline, up to and including discharge. Yours very truly, ABC Inc.

CHAPTER 6: SAMPLE DISCIPLINARY LETTERS

6.1 — Introduction

Sample disciplinary letters dealing with a variety of circumstances are found on the following pages. Please note that these letters are provided as guides only. In every case, both the form and content of the disciplinary letter will depend on the particular circumstances. In each case, however, the disciplinary letter should generally contain the main elements set out in the previous chapter. Once again, those elements are:

- the disciplinary record;
- the infraction;
- the disciplinary penalty;
- available employee support; and
- notice.

6.2 — Sample Letters

a) — Suspension for fighting

Dear Ms Jones:

Re: One-day suspension

We have completed our investigation into the events of January 10.

It is clear that on January 10 you engaged in a physical altercation with your fellow employee, Ms Jane Smith. As a result of the altercation, both you and Ms Smith required medical attention.

Physical altercations endanger the health and safety of ABC Inc.'s employees and customers. Such acts are unacceptable to ABC Inc. and your misconduct will not be tolerated.

To ensure that you understand the seriousness of your misconduct, we have no choice but to issue this one (1) day suspension without pay effective January 15. You will return to work on January 16.

We trust that this discipline will correct your behaviour in the future. However, if you engage in further misconduct of any kind, you may be subject to more severe discipline up to and including discharge.

Yours very truly,

ABC Inc.
c.c. Personnel File
[union representative — if required/applicable]

b) — Warning for unauthorized absence from work

Dear Ms Brown:

Re: Written warning

On October 10, you failed to report for your scheduled shift at 9:00 a.m. You did not notify your manager of your absence in advance. Furthermore, upon your return to work on October 11, you failed to provide a justifiable excuse for your absence or your failure to notify your manager in advance. This conduct is unacceptable and will not be tolerated by ABC Inc.

A review of your record indicates that you have failed to report to work without notice or justifiable excuse on several occasions in the past. In the past 12 months alone, you were absent in this manner on two (2) other occasions. These absences were on June 1 and September 15. On both of those occasions, you were given verbal warnings and directed to notify your manager in advance of every absence.

In light of the foregoing, we have no choice but to issue this written warning. We trust that this discipline will ensure that you correct your behaviour in the future.

However, please note that if you engage in further misconduct of any kind, you may be subject to more severe discipline, up to and including suspensions and discharge.

Yours very truly,

ABC Inc.
c.c. Personnel File
[union representative — if required/applicable]

c) — Suspension for unauthorized absence from work

Dear Mr. Johnson:

Re: One-day suspension

Following our warnings of January 15 and February 12 regarding your unauthorized absences from work, it has come to our attention that you have not improved your behaviour.

You were absent from work without notification and without justifiable excuse on March 25 and 30.

ABC Inc. believes that you are capable of improving your behaviour. As you have been made aware in the past, you must notify your manager in advance of every absence.

In light of the foregoing, we have no choice but to issue this one (1) day suspension without pay effective April 2. You will return to work on April 3.

We trust that you will now correct your behaviour. However, if you engage in further misconduct of any kind, you may be subject to more severe discipline up to and including discharge.

Yours very truly,

ABC Inc.

c.c. Personnel File

[union representative — if required/applicable]

d) — Suspension for theft

Dear Mr. Thompson:

Re: Five-day suspension

We have completed our investigation into the events of June 1.

We have determined that on June 1 you stole Mr. Bob Smith's wristwatch from his locker at ABC Inc.'s facility. You returned the watch during the course of our investigation on June 7.

This misconduct is unacceptable and will not be tolerated by ABC Inc. under any circumstances. As honesty is vital to any viable employment relationship, theft is one of the most serious forms of misconduct in an employment relationship.

To ensure that you understand the seriousness of your misconduct, we have no choice but to issue this five (5) day suspension without pay effective June 12. You will return to work on June 19.

Please note that this suspension represents a final warning. If you engage in further misconduct of any kind, you will be discharged.

Yours very truly,

ABC Inc.

c.c. Personnel File
[union representative — if required/applicable]

e) — Dismissal for damaging company property

Dear Mr. Franklin:

Re: Dismissal

We have completed our investigation into the events of April 10.

It is clear that on April 10, immediately following a verbal disagreement with your supervisor, Joe Williams, you wilfully damaged four computers belonging to ABC Inc. The estimated cost of the damage you caused is more than $12,000.00.

This misconduct is unacceptable and will not be tolerated by ABC Inc.

Accordingly, we have no choice but to terminate your employment effective immediately. We regret having to take this action, however, your misconduct leaves us with no alternative.

All outstanding vacation pay and other employee entitlements, if any, will be provided to you within the next seven days.

Yours very truly,

ABC Inc.

c.c. Personnel File
[union representative — if required/applicable]

f) — Warning for failure to adhere to safety policies

Dear Mr. Clark:

Re: Written Warning

You were verbally warned on February 5 and February 7 about the necessity of wearing protective eyewear in accordance with the applicable health and safety regulation. Despite those warnings, you have continually refused to wear your safety glasses as required.

This misconduct is unacceptable. Adherence to health and safety regulations is necessary to ensure the well being of all ABC Inc.'s employees. We are also under a statutory duty to take every precaution reasonable for the safety of both yourself and your co-workers. If your safety glasses are damaged or do not fit properly, please bring this to the attention of your supervisor.

In light of the foregoing, we have no choice but to issue this written warning. This discipline is intended to ensure that, in the future, you comply with all health and safety regulations and policies, including those requiring protective eyewear.

We are confident that you will comply with all such regulations in the future. Please be advised, however, that if you engage in further misconduct of any kind, you may be subject to more severe discipline up to and including suspension or discharge.

Yours very truly,

ABC Inc.

c.c. Personnel File

[union representative — if required/applicable]

Chapter 7: The Disciplinary and Discharge Meetings

7.1 — Introduction

Following completion of the investigation and a decision to take disciplinary action, the employer should prepare a disciplinary or discharge letter to present to the employee and the union, if any, as soon as possible. The issuance of discipline typically takes place at a disciplinary meeting. Where such a meeting is neither possible nor practicable, the disciplinary or discharge letter may be couriered to the employee.

In unionized settings, the collective agreement often sets out procedural requirements that must be observed by the employer when preparing for a disciplinary meeting. For example, the collective agreement may address such issues as union representation, time limits, and notice requirements. If a mandatory procedure in the collective agreement is not followed, an arbitrator may, depending on the contractual language, later rescind the discipline imposed at the meeting.

A properly conducted disciplinary meeting should be brief and to the point. In order to accomplish this, an employer must prepare for the meeting well in advance.

7.2 — Tone

An employer should be very direct when conducting a disciplinary meeting. The employer should quickly get to the point of the meeting and avoid trying to establish a rapport by engaging in "small talk". The employer should also avoid the temptation to defend its decision or argue about it. The meeting should not become confrontational. An employer should maintain a polite but firm tone throughout the disciplinary meeting. Discipline that is administered in any other manner may lower the employee's sense of self-worth and will generally be less effective.

It is vital that an employer refrain from utilizing the disciplinary procedure as a tool for dealing with the employer's frustration with, or even anger at, a particular employee. Discipline resulting from such an emotional response is far less likely to achieve the legitimate goals of discipline.

7.3 — Clarity and Completeness

During the meeting, the employer should clearly identify the discipline being imposed and the reasons for it. Otherwise, the employee may be unsure or unaware that he or she has been disciplined or may not fully understand the reasons for the discipline.

The employer should ensure that all the grounds for the discipline are clearly communicated to the employee, both in writing and verbally during the disciplinary meeting. If an employer has three specific reasons for dismissing an employee, but only refers to one of those reasons, it may appear to an arbitrator or court which subsequently reviews the matter that the employer was fabricating the other two reasons.

Traditionally, at common law, an employer was not required to give an employee reasons for dismissal. More recently, some courts have required employers to allow employees to respond to allegations of just cause. A failure to provide an employee with reasons for dismissal may be found to constitute evidence that the employer's actions were not in good faith and may create a rebuttable presumption that the dismissal was not warranted. As a practical matter, regardless of whether just cause for dismissal is being asserted, an employer should clearly explain to the employee why he or she is being released, if the employment is being terminated.

7.4 — Witnesses

In addition to the manager or supervisor who will administer the disciplinary penalty, a second manager/supervisor or human resources representative should be present during the disciplinary meeting. This second person serves as a witness. The witness should be advised of how the interview will proceed and should be instructed to remain quiet, listen and observe the events at the meeting. Most importantly, the witness should take detailed notes during the meeting.

Having a witness is invaluable if the employee later challenges the disciplinary penalty and the events at the disciplinary meeting.

7.5 — Timing

It is preferable to schedule a disciplinary meeting at the end of the workday (or even after normal working hours, depending on the requirements of any collective agreement). This timing lessens the likelihood of the employee being embarrassed in front of his or her co-workers. Such a strategy also limits the employee's opportunity to disparage the employer in front of other employees before having an opportunity to reflect upon the disciplinary penalty.

As a general rule, it is preferable to discharge employees before the end of the week so as to enable them the opportunity to immediately apply for employment insurance and commence a search for alternative employment.

7.6 — Location

The meeting should be conducted in a private office or boardroom. Disciplining an employee in front of other employees is inappropriate and likely to cause unnecessary humiliation.

To avoid the difficulties that may arise if the employee refuses to leave at the conclusion of the meeting, employers often choose not to hold disciplinary meetings in managers' or supervisors' offices. By choosing a conference room or other neutral area where the employee can be left, the manager or supervisor can control the length of the meeting by leaving when it is over.

7.7 — The Offer to Resign

During disciplinary meetings, employees sometimes offer to resign in order to avoid being dismissed. An employee may make such an offer where the dismissal is based on serious grounds such as theft or fraud and the employee realizes the difficulties that he or she could face obtaining employment after such a dismissal.

To be valid, the resignation must be voluntary and free from coercion by the employer. The employee must also have a subjective intention to resign. If the employee's alleged resignation is the result of the employee being in a state of shock, anger, fear, or frustration, the validity of the resignation may later be called into question.

Consequently, employers who are faced with a resignation during a disciplinary meeting should advise the employee that they are prepared to accept the resignation. However, the employee should be counselled to take some time (e.g. a few days) to reflect on the resignation. This period of reflection will ensure that the resignation is truly voluntary. Once the employee confirms his or her intention to resign in this manner, the employer should obtain a written resignation. This may be used as evidence in any future legal proceeding; at the very least, confirm acceptance of the employee's decision to resign in writing to the employee. The employee should be advised that the disciplinary meeting will be suspended on a without prejudice basis pending his or her consideration of the proposed resignation.

7.8 — Following Up After the Disciplinary Meeting

Where discipline other than discharge is imposed, the employer should generally conduct a follow-up investigation to assess the effectiveness of the disciplinary penalty, particularly in cases involving serious employee misconduct. The follow-up investigation should include efforts to maintain a good working relationship between the supervisor and the employee who was disciplined.

After disciplining an employee, a manager or supervisor may avoid the employee or subtly alter his or her attitude towards the employee. These shifts in attitude often generate corresponding alterations in the employee's attitude. If left unchecked, the relationship between the manager or supervisor and the employee may be jeopardized. By contrast, if the employee is treated in the same manner, the previous relationship will likely be maintained and hopefully even improved.

Managerial personnel should be reminded that once an employee has received a disciplinary penalty, the employee should not continue to be punished for the earlier misconduct. Rather, the employee should be given an opportunity to demonstrate that he or she has learned from the experience. It is vital that the employer make a sincere effort to ensure that positive, rather than negative, results are achieved from the disciplinary response.

7.9 — The Termination Meeting

Most of the same principles apply to both disciplinary and termination meetings. The key objective of a termination meeting is to communicate the decision to terminate the employment in a humane but clear manner. The employer representatives should avoid saying or doing anything which might give rise to a claim that the termination was conducted in bad faith or in an unduly harsh or insensitive manner. The following is a simple checklist for conducting termination meetings.

1. Structure of Meeting and Confidentiality

- Comply with applicable collective agreement provisions regarding notice and union representation.
- Two persons should conduct the meeting on behalf of the employer.
- Following the meeting, careful notes should be made of the discussion.
- The meeting should be conducted in a private office or boardroom out of the earshot of other individuals.
- The termination should not be communicated to others in the organization until the employee has had an opportunity to inform colleagues, if he so desires.
- The employee should be given an opportunity to remove personal effects after hours or over the weekend when other employees are not present.
- The employee should be given an opportunity to return the Employer's property at some mutually convenient time. (It is sometimes a mistake for employers to simply demand the employee's keys and credit cards and escort the employee directly from the workplace.)

2. Be Direct

- Avoid trying to establish rapport by engaging in small talk.
- Quickly get to the point of the meeting, then move directly into the specifics.
- The meeting should last no longer than 10-15 minutes.

3. State the Reason for the Termination

- Clearly indicate the reason for the decision.
- Ensure that statements made are consistent with legal positions the employer may take to defend a resulting grievance or wrongful dismissal action.
- If the employer will allege just cause, indicate that the dismissal results from the employee's conduct or performance.
- Normally, the employment termination and reasons (where the employer is alleging just cause) should be confirmed in a letter delivered to the employee during or subsequent to the meeting.

4. Be Clear on the Actions Being Taken

- Be certain the individual completely understands that he or she has been discharged and that the decision is irrevocable.
- For non-union employees, clearly communicate any proposal for settlement or options (e.g. resignation, early retirement). Alternatively, clearly communicate the process for settlement. For unionized employees, settlements must be negotiated with the union.

5. Don't Get Defensive

- Resist the temptation to defend and argue about the decision or the rationale for it. (No matter what is said, nothing will satisfy the terminated employee.)
- Do not allow the meeting to become confrontational.
- Do not threaten or imply that the employee will receive a negative reference or a lesser settlement if the employee indicates that he will take legal action.

6. Avoid Platitudes and Promises

- Refrain from statements such as "This really isn't the worst thing that could happen to you".
- Avoid giving false hope and volunteering advice related to potential employment or future alternatives.

7.10 — After a Dismissal

Special considerations arise where a disciplinary meeting is conducted for the purpose of discharging an employee.

a) — Personal items

Employers often require a dismissed employee to remove his or her personal possessions from the workplace immediately after the disciplinary meeting. If possible, it is preferable to give the employee the opportunity to remove any personal possessions after hours or over the weekend when other employees are not present. It is also preferable for a manager or supervisor other than the one who conducted the termination meeting to accompany the employee when he or she collects his or her possessions. Having someone uninvolved in the termination meeting accompany the employee reduces the likelihood of unnecessary discussions and potentially unpleasant scenes. It is important that a dismissed employee should not be left alone in the workplace after the dismissal meeting.

b) — References

It generally does not serve the interests of an employer to prevent a dismissed employee from obtaining subsequent employment. At common law, a non-unionized employee has a duty to mitigate any damages flowing from the employee's wrongful dismissal. Accordingly, in many legal proceedings, where an employee's dismissal is found to be without just cause or reasonable notice, compensation earned by the employee through alternative employment subsequent to the dismissal may be deducted from the damages otherwise due to the employee. Consequently, the amount ultimately payable by the employer to the employee could be increased if the employer hinders the employee's efforts to find alternate employment. Furthermore, a refusal to provide a reference has, in some circumstances, been found to constitute bad faith and may result in an extension of the reasonable notice period for discharging a non-union employee.

By no means, however, should an employer misrepresent the employee to prospective employers. The employer could potentially be found liable for any such misrepresentations. Additionally, if the employer alleged just cause for the employee's discharge, any overly positive reference letters may be used as evidence against the employer in future legal proceedings.

The solution, therefore, is for the employer to be neutral and objective. At the very least, information such as the employee's length of service, positions held, and duties and responsibilities can usually be given. Whether an employer will or can go further will depend upon all surrounding circumstances. An employer's actions may also be constrained by any applicable policies, such as a formal policy not to discuss the circumstances surrounding an employee's departure. Potential employers can then be advised of that policy.

c) — Other employees

Before announcing the dismissal of an employee, the employer should give the employee an opportunity to inform colleagues if he or she so desires. An employer must, however, announce the dismissal to other employees within a reasonably short time after it occurs. The reason for the dismissal should be set out in a concise and factual manner that does not unnecessarily tarnish the employee's reputation or hinder the employee's efforts to obtain subsequent employment. In some situations, the parties will negotiate the content and form of the announcement regarding the employee's termination of employment.

Where an employer does not provide other employees with any kind of information, employees may come to their own (often inaccurate) conclusions regarding the reasons for the dismissal. The resulting rumours will often have a negative effect on employees' morale.

d) — Post-discharge obligations

Absent contractual provisions limiting an employee's ability to compete with his or her former employer or limiting his or her right to solicit the client's of a former employer, employers have relatively few common law protections. Generally speaking, former employees are permitted to engage in "fair competition" with their former employer, which includes setting up a rival business and using the knowledge and skills acquired during the course of their employment.

One protection that is afforded to employers is the law's recognition that a company has a proprietary interest in its confidential information even in the absence of a contractual provision governing confidentiality. The courts will protect companies from the unauthorized use and disclosure of their proprietary confidential information. The duty of confidence lasts until the information is no longer confidential. In order to succeed in a breach of confidence action, an employer would have to establish the following elements set out in *International Corona Resources Ltd. v. LAC Minerals Ltd.*, 1989 CarswellOnt 965, 1989 CarswellOnt 126, 26 C.P.R. (3d) 97, [1989] 2 S.C.R. 574, 61 D.L.R. (4th) 14 (S.C.C.): that the information conveyed was confidential; that it was communicated in confidence; and that it was misused by the party to whom it was communicated. Pricing information has been found to not be confidential information. However, information about customers and customer lists is generally found to constitute confidential information unless it is not treated as being confidential.

In addition to prohibiting the improper use of confidential information, the law imposes special obligations on fiduciary employees. To be a fiduciary, an employee must meet the following criteria:

1. The fiduciary has scope for the exercise of some discretion or power.

2. The fiduciary can unilaterally exercise that power or discretion so as to affect the beneficiary's legal or practical interests.

3. The beneficiary is peculiarly vulnerable to or at the mercy of the fiduciary holding the discretion or power.

A fiduciary duty typically applies to directors and senior managers of an organization. However, key employees can also be found to owe a fiduciary duty to their employers. Key employees can include lower level employees who exercise substantial management functions. To determine if an employee owes a fiduciary duty to his or her employer, it is necessary to examine the reasonable expectations of the employee and the employer in the context of factors such as trust, confidence, the nature of the employee's position and community or industry standards.

The Supreme Court of Canada described the duties arising from the fiduciary relationship in the seminal case of *Canadian Aero Service Ltd. v. O'Malley* (1973), 1973 CarswellOnt 236F, 1973 CarswellOnt 236, 11 C.P.R. (2d) 206, 40 D.L.R. (3d) 371, [1974] S.C.R. 592 (S.C.C.) as follows at pages 381 to 382 [D.L.R.]:

> [I]n its generality [the fiduciary relationship] betokens loyalty, good faith and avoidance of a conflict of duty and self-interest. Descending from the generality, the fiduciary relationship goes at least this far: a director or

senior officer ... is precluded from obtaining for himself, either secretly or without the approval of the company (which would have to be properly manifested upon full disclosure of the facts), any property or business advantage either belonging to the company or for which it has been negotiating; and especially is this so where the director or officer is a participant in the negotiations on behalf of the company.

At common law, a number of fiduciary duties exist including:

1. A duty to not directly or indirectly solicit any of the former employer's business or customers;

2. A duty to not usurp any corporate business opportunities rightfully belonging to the employer;

3. A duty to not directly or indirectly solicit any of the former employer's employees, including causing such individuals to work for a new employer, or a new business started by the employee; and

4. A duty to not use, disclose or seek to obtain any confidential materials, information or trade secrets belonging to the former employer, and a duty to return to the former employer any such information.

A breach of an employee's fiduciary duty can occur where any of the above-noted duties is not respected. In certain circumstances, where an employer has commenced an action against a former employee for breach of fiduciary duty, a court can grant an injunction to stop the employee from continuing to breach his or her duty awaiting the outcome of the legal proceedings.

Given the rather limited protections afforded to employers faced with competition from former employees who are not fiduciaries, it is generally advisable to have employees, particularly key employees and executives, sign confidentiality agreements and, where appropriate, non-solicitation agreements prior to commencing employment. Each agreement should be tailored to the particular circumstances of the individual employee. Employees may be asked to sign a non-competition agreement where a non-solicitation agreement would not be sufficient. Non-competition agreements will not be enforced by the courts where a non-solicitation agreement is sufficient to protect the company's legitimate interests. The agreement should be limited to a reasonable geographical area in the context of the industry. The geographical area should be large enough to protect the company's interests but small enough to be enforceable by the courts. For example, where it is sufficient to apply the non-solicitation ban to the City of Toronto, the court will not uphold a ban that applies to the Province of Ontario. The agreement should impose the non-solicitation and/or non-competition ban for a reasonable period of time in the context of the nature of the employer's business and the employee's position (e.g. one year). Any such agreements should be brought to the employee's attention at the time of employment termination. Finally, prompt action should be taken in response to any breach of such an agreement or of a fiduciary duty.

Significant Case Law

RBC Dominion Securities Inc. v. Merrill Lynch Canada Inc., 2008 CarswellBC 2100, 2008 CarswellBC 2099, 298 D.L.R. (4th) 1, 84 B.C.L.R. (4th) 1, [2008] 3 S.C.R. 79 (S.C.C.)

In RBC Dominion Securities, the Supreme Court of Canada found that non-fiduciary employees may not be held liable simply for competing with their former employer during the reasonable notice period.

The Facts

In Cranbrook, British Columbia, RBC and Merrill Lynch were each other's main competitors in the investment advice market. RBC's branch manager, Don Delamont, was good friends with James Michaud, who had become Merrill Lynch's regional manager after working with RBC and its predecessors for almost twenty years. It appears that Delamont and Michaud had an axe to grind with RBC as they, with help from Merrill Lynch, managed to orchestrate a mass exodus of employees.

In November 2000, Delamont, along with virtually all of the investment advisors employed by RBC Securities Inc. at its Cranbrook office, left their employment with RBC and immediately started working for Merrill Lynch. The only people who did not transfer were two members of the support staff and a pair of junior investment advisors, who were not asked to be part of the move. Michaud worked closely with Delamont in planning the move, including actively recruiting all of the employees who made the transfer. No advance notice of the decision to defect was provided to RBC by the investment advisors.

The evidence disclosed that prior to the move to Merrill Lynch, RBC's confidential client records had been surreptitiously copied and transferred to its competitor.

Not surprisingly, RBC's Cranbrook office all but collapsed as a result of the defections. In response, RBC sued Merrill Lynch, Michaud, Delamont and the former investment advisors, claiming damages for breach of fiduciary duty, breach of an implied duty not to compete unfairly upon leaving RBC, failure to provide reasonable notice, misuse of confidential information (against Delamont and the other former employees), inducing breach of contract (against Merrill Lynch, Michaud and Delamont), and conspiracy and conversion (against all of the defendants). Notably, none of the employees who made the switch to Merrill Lynch had any restrictive covenants in their employment contracts.

The Decision

At trial, Holmes J. of the British Columbia Supreme Court allowed the action, but dismissed the claims for conspiracy and breach of fiduciary duty against the employees. He held that no such duties were owed to RBC. However, the Court found that the employees had failed to provide reasonable notice of resignation and had competed unfairly with RBC by engaging in concerted efforts to transfer clients and by removing confidential client information before RBC could protect its business relationships. All of the remaining claims against Merrill Lynch, Michaud and Delamont were allowed.

At a second stage of the trial, Holmes J. assessed damages for the wrongs committed by the various defendants. The largest part of the damages award (almost $1.5 million) was against the orchestrator, Delamont, for the loss of profits associated with the breach of his duty of good faith. However, the investment advisors were also found liable, in the amount of $40,000 each, for a failure to give reasonable notice of resignation, as well as a total of $225,000 for RBC's lost profits due to their unfair competition. Merrill Lynch and Michaud were also held jointly and severally liable for those damages (and an additional $250,000 in punitive damages).

On appeal to the B.C. Court of Appeal, the Court was divided on the assessment of damages. The majority of the Court overturned the substantial damages award against Delamont, as well as the damages ordered against the former employees for profits lost due to the unfair competition, but upheld the other damages awarded.

With respect to the claim against Delamont, the Supreme Court of Canada found that the damages awarded by the trial judge were consistent with the claims pled against Delamont. The Supreme Court found that it would have been in the contemplation of RBC and Delamont, at the time of entering into the employment contract, that Delamont would be liable for the lost profits if he were to orchestrate the departure of almost all of the branch's investment advisors. The use of a five year window for calculating the lost profits was found to be reasonable and supported by the evidence at trial.

With respect to the investment advisors' liability for "unfair competition", the Supreme Court ruled that the damages awarded could not stand. The Supreme Court found that once the employees left their employment with RBC, they were subject to some residual duties but were free to compete with RBC. At paragraphs 18 through 20, the Supreme Court stated:

> The majority of the Court of Appeal ... held that once the investment advisors left RBC, they were no longer under a duty not to compete with it. The view of the Court of Appeal on the law for the purposes of this issue may be summed up as follows. Generally, an employee who has terminated employment is not prevented from competing with his or her employer during the notice period, and the employer is confined to damages for failure to give reasonable notice (Southin J.A. for the majority). To this general proposition Rowles J.A. may be read as adding the qualification that a departing employee might be liable for specific wrongs such as improper use of confidential information during the notice period. This appears to be consistent with the current law, which restricts post-employment duties to the duty not to misuse confidential information, as well as duties arising out of a fiduciary duty or restrictive covenant: [citations omitted]. Neither of the latter duties are at issue here.
>
> For the purposes of this case, the law may be accepted as summarized by the preceding paragraph. The contract of employment ends when either the employer or the employee terminates the employment relationship, although residual duties may remain. An employee terminating his or her employment may be liable for failure to give reasonable notice and for breach of specific residual duties. Subject to these duties, the employee is free to compete against the former employer.
>
> To the extent the trial judge awarded damages on the basis that the employees continued to be under a general duty not to compete, this award of damages was wrong in law.

Accordingly, the appeal was allowed in part. The trial judge's decision was reinstated in respect of Delamont, while the Court of Appeal's decision denying damages for unfair competition was upheld.

The Implications

While it may seem inherently improper for employees leaving one employer to be permitted to immediately commence working with a direct competitor, the Supreme Court of Canada's decision is clear that former employees are not prohibited from doing so, even where they have not provided reasonable notice of resignation.

Employers who may be vulnerable to mass defections should ensure that they include post-termination obligations in the employment contracts of those employees whose departures could harm the bottom line, as well as provisions dealing with the enforcement of such duties. This can be accomplished by way of restrictive covenants. In the absence of provisions that survive the end of the employment relationship, employers may be left with little recourse when departing employees take the business with them.

While it is recommended that employers include appropriate restrictive covenants in all employment contracts, it should be noted that restrictive covenants, especially non-competition clauses, can be very difficult to enforce, as they are often viewed by the courts as an inappropriate restraint on trade. Accordingly, restrictive covenants must be drafted very carefully to maximize the potential that they will be upheld by the courts.

The Supreme Court did reinforce that employees are required to provide reasonable notice of resignation, similar to an employer's requirement to provide reasonable notice when terminating one or more of its employees. The employees in the instant case were held liable for their failure to provide reasonable notice of resignation, thereby leaving RBC in a position where it all but collapsed. While the Supreme Court upheld the requirement for reasonable notice of resignation, the best practice remains to include specific notice of resignation periods in each employment contract.

The Supreme Court of Canada's decision also confirms that employees, whether in a fiduciary role or not, may not misuse their employer's confidential information. This decision also confirms that managers owe a duty of good faith to their employer.

Significant Case Law

KJA Consultants Inc. v. Soberman, 2003 CarswellOnt 3065, 36 B.L.R. (3d) 19 (Ont. S.C.J.), additional reasons at (2003), 2003 CarswellOnt 3791 (Ont. S.C.J.), affirmed (2004), 2004 CarswellOnt 4576, 50 B.L.R. (3d) 283 (Ont. C.A.)

KJA Consultants suggests that a fiduciary employee's duty to not solicit his or her former employer's customers extends to also prohibit the employee from accepting solicitations initiated by the customers.

The Facts

KJA commenced an action against Soberman after he resigned and set up his own business in competition with KJA. KJA alleged that Soberman solicited its customers and took over a project with one of its largest clients, Great West Life ("GWL").

Soberman was employed with KJA for 13 years, spending his final four years with the company as its general manager. As general manager, Soberman was responsible for marketing and sales, liaising with KJA's board of directors, client contact, managing KJA employees across Canada and KJA's overall performance. Essentially, Soberman was the "face" of KJA and was a key employee.

Prior to Soberman's departure, KJA learned of his intention to set up a competing business and reminded Soberman of his duties to not use KJA's confidential information, to not appropriate any of KJA's corporate opportunities that arose while he was employed with KJA and to not solicit or contact KJA's customers for a period of 12 months.

Nonetheless, in the process of establishing his business, Soberman sent letters to approximately 400 of KJA's current and past customers.

Prior to Soberman's departure, he was involved in a substantial ongoing project that KJA was performing for GWL. Soberman did not send a solicitation letter to GWL or solicit GWL in any way. However, once GWL learned of Soberman's departure, it contacted Soberman and advised him that it preferred that he complete the project instead of KJA. GWL requested that Soberman submit a proposal to take over the project from KJA. Soberman agreed.

The Decision

While Soberman had not signed a non-competition or non-solicitation agreement with KJA, the Court determined that Soberman breached his fiduciary duty to KJA when he accepted GWL's offer to complete the project. In particular, the Court found that Soberman's knowledge of the project was entirely as a result of his employment with KJA. Soberman breached his fiduciary duty when he used this knowledge to take the project away from KJA.

The Court also found Soberman breached his fiduciary duty by soliciting and commencing projects with a number of KJA's other customers. The non-solicitation ban was imposed on Soberman for 12 months following his departure from KJA.

The Court ordered Soberman to pay damages to KJA for the loss of the GWL project. Soberman was also required to compensate KJA for the profit he received for projects completed with other customers that he solicited from KJA.

The Implications

The KJA Consultants decision represents a possible shift in the law in Ontario. The law has long held that key or senior management employees subject to fiduciary duties may not solicit their former employer's customer(s) for a reasonable period of time. However, the KJA Consultants decision suggests that an employee may breach his or her fiduciary duty even where the customer solicits the employee.

7.11 — Maintaining Employee Disciplinary Records

After discipline is imposed, the employer should update all disciplinary records. As stated earlier, the doctrine of the culminating incident allows an employer to review an employee's previous record any time the employee's conduct calls for the imposition of discipline (subject to any collective agreement restrictions). In other words, where the final incident of misconduct does not warrant the severity of the penalty imposed, the employer may rely on the employee's prior disciplinary record to justify that penalty. For this reason, disciplinary records are important for determining the appropriate discipline.

In unionized environments, grievance files should be maintained for at least three further reasons. First, a grievance settled through the arbitration process may be the subject of an application for judicial review. Second, the information in the grievance file may be necessary to establish a *res judicata* defence in the event that the employee or union attempts to file a second grievance based on the same grounds. *Res judicata* is a legal doctrine that prevents a party from advancing a claim if it has already obtained a decision in a previous claim dealing with precisely the same subject matter. In order for *res judicata* to apply, the earlier decision must relate to the same issue, a final judgment must have been reached, and the same parties must be involved. Similarly, a grievance file may be used to establish an issue estoppel defence in another proceeding (e.g. an employment standards or human rights inquiry). Issue estoppel is a legal doctrine that bars a party from litigating an issue that has already been decided against that party in the context of a previous claim. Finally, disciplinary records may be relevant to establishing consistency of treatment in respect of similar misconduct by another employee.

With respect to how long records should be maintained, collective agreements often contain sunset clauses, which provide that disciplinary records will be disregarded and/or removed from the employee's file after a given period of time. Subject to the requirements of the collective agreement, it is generally advisable to maintain complete personnel files, including disciplinary records, for the duration of the employment relationship and for a number of years thereafter.

Disciplinary records should be maintained even following an employee's dismissal. Claims by unionized employees must be brought within the relevant time limits prescribed in the collective agreement. The personnel records of unionized employees should be retained at least until the expiration of those time limits. In addition, a variety of statutes regulate records retention. For example, the *Employment Standards Act, 2000* requires an employer to keep certain records regarding an employee for three years after the employee ceases employment with the employer.

The personnel records of non-unionized employees may be relevant to the pursuit or defence of a civil claim such as a claim for damages for wrongful dismissal. Previously, actions for breach of contract or tort had to be brought within six years after the cause of action arose. However, Ontario's current limitations legislation (the *Limitations Act, 2002*), which came into force on January 1, 2004, establishes a basic limitation period of two years, running from the day the "claim" is "discovered". A "claim" is defined as "a claim to remedy an injury, loss or damage that occurred as a result of an act or omission". Accordingly, under the *Limitations Act, 2002*, a plaintiff will generally be barred from commencing a lawsuit claiming breach of contract or tortious conduct after the second anniversary of the day on which the claim was discovered (e.g. the date that the employee was given his or her notice of termination). Generally speaking, all personnel records should be retained for at least as long as necessary to ensure compliance with any statutory requirements and the relevant statutory limitation period.

Part III: Additional Considerations

Chapter 8: Collective Agreement Clauses

8.1 — Introduction

In unionized workplaces, collective agreements govern many of the aspects of the disciplinary procedure. An employer must be completely familiar with all the relevant clauses of the collective agreement before imposing any disciplinary penalty. Failure to comply with such clauses could ultimately lead to the penalty being overturned.

8.2 — Sample Clauses

No two collective agreements are identical. Nevertheless, most collective agreements contain variations of certain key clauses that relate to the disciplinary and discharge procedure.

a) — Just cause

One of the most fundamental provisions in most collective agreements is the requirement that the employer only discipline or discharge an employee for just cause. A typical just cause provision is as follows:

> The employer shall not discipline or discharge any employee except for just cause.

Subject to the collective agreement's lay-off procedures, one of the effects of a just cause provision is to prevent an employer from discharging an employee merely by giving the employee reasonable notice or pay in lieu thereof.

Where the parties have included a just cause provision in their collective agreement and the union challenges a disciplinary penalty at arbitration, the employer will bear the burden of establishing that it had just cause to impose the penalty. If just cause cannot be established, an arbitrator may rescind the discipline.

b) — Timeliness

Many collective agreements provide that an employer must impose a disciplinary penalty within a specified time from the occurrence of the alleged infraction or the date the employer became aware of it. If the employer delays in imposing the disciplinary penalty, the penalty may be found to be void. An example of a clause dealing with such a time limit is as follows:

> The employer shall only impose a disciplinary penalty on an employee within twenty (20) days of the occurrence of the alleged infraction or within twenty (20) days of the date upon which the employer became aware of it, whichever is later.

A time period that runs from the date the employer is aware of the alleged infraction generally begins when one of the employer's managerial employees, including managers, supervisors, and even foremen, becomes aware of the incident. As such, all such managerial employees should be trained to respond appropriately to disciplinary events, including knowing which member of management should be notified in various circumstances.

c) — Presence of a union representative

Whenever administering a disciplinary penalty, an employer should ensure that any requirement in the collective agreement regarding the presence of a union representative is observed. Examples of typical union representation clauses are as follows:

> An employee shall be entitled to have a union representative present at any meeting at which the employee may be disciplined or discharged.
>
> — or —
>
> At the beginning of any disciplinary interview, the employer shall inform the employee being disciplined that he or she is entitled to have a union representative present. Failure by the employer to so inform the employee shall render any discipline subsequently rendered invalid.

If an employer proceeds with a disciplinary interview without allowing an employee to have a union representative present, the employer risks having any discipline imposed later declared invalid. However, in certain circumstances, an employer may be able to hold a second disciplinary interview at which it ensures that a union representative is present. If the employee has been prejudiced by the earlier failure or the time limit for imposing discipline has expired, this option may not be available to the employer.

d) — Issuing reasons

Many collective agreements provide that when suspending or dismissing an employee, the employer must provide the employee with the reasons for its decision. Two examples of such a provision are the following:

> The employer shall provide an employee who is to be suspended or dismissed with a written notice of the suspension or dismissal setting out the reasons for such disciplinary penalty. The employer shall provide such written notice to the employee as well as to the union, within one (1) working day of the suspension or discharge.
>
> — or —
>
> An employee who is to be disciplined or dismissed shall be provided with a written notice of the discipline at the time the discipline is imposed. The written notice shall set out the basis for the discipline being imposed.

It is important for employers to accurately set out the grounds for the suspension or discharge in the disciplinary letter. If an employer fails to include certain grounds, it may be prevented from relying on them, unless the grounds are related to the original reasons or were not known at the time the disciplinary penalty was issued.

e) — Reviewing personnel files

Some collective agreements provide that employees are entitled to review their personnel files upon giving reasonable notice to the employer. Two examples of such a clause are the following:

> An employee shall be entitled to review his or her personnel file in the presence of the employer, upon giving reasonable notice to the employer. The employee shall also be entitled to receive copies of documents in the file, as reasonably requested.

— or —

> The employer shall permit any employee to review his or her personnel file and to receive copies of records contained in the file. The employee shall be entitled to have his or her comments with respect to any record in the file added to the file.

Such a clause enables the employee to ensure that he or she is aware of all the documentation upon which the employer may rely in any disciplinary proceeding. This awareness provides the employee with an opportunity to challenge any information in the file. If an employer denies this right to an employee or fails to keep all appropriate documentation in an employee's personnel file, the employer may be prevented from relying upon the personnel file, or portions thereof, at a future proceeding.

f) — Sunset clauses

In many instances, an employer will establish just cause for discipline by demonstrating that, in addition to the culminating incident, the employee had a history of other infractions. An employer's ability to rely on the employee's past history, or disciplinary record, will often depend on whether the collective agreement contains a "sunset clause" (also sometimes called a "cleansing" provision).

A sunset clause requires references to previous disciplinary penalties to be removed from an employee's record after a certain time has elapsed. Two examples of sunset clauses are as follows:

> All disciplinary measures taken against an employee shall be removed from the employee's file after a period of twelve (12) months following the date of the alleged infraction.

— or —

> When disciplining an employee, the employer shall not take into account any disciplinary measures taken against the employee twelve (12) months prior to the date of the alleged infraction.

Some sunset clauses apply only if the employee does not receive any discipline during the stipulated period. For example:

> All written records of warnings and suspensions shall be withdrawn from an employee's file after twelve (12) months from the date of the last written record, provided that no further written records have been issued to the employee in the twelve (12) month period.

In certain circumstances, sunset clauses make it more difficult for an employer to apply progressive discipline to manage an employee's behaviour. For example, an employee may space his or her disciplinary events apart over extended periods of time. With the expiration of each sunset period, the employee is deemed to have a clean disciplinary record and the employer may not rely upon the previous disciplinary events. Often, however, an employee's record is cleared in part because the employer failed to properly monitor the employee's behaviour and issue timely disciplinary responses. All employers must be vigilant in ensuring that disciplinary penalties are imposed in a timely manner, but especially where there is the added impact of a sunset clause.

g) — Non-discrimination clause

Many collective agreements contain a non-discrimination clause. In general, the purpose of a non-discrimination clause is to expressly prohibit discrimination against employees by either the employer or the union based on either human rights grounds or union status.

An example is:

> The parties must not discriminate against any Employee because of age, race, colour, creed, ancestry, place of origin, citizenship, sex, ethic origin, sexual orientation, disability or because of membership or non-membership or activity in the Union.

With respect to human rights, the Supreme Court of Canada (see the *Parry Sound* decision) has confirmed that whether or not a collective agreement contains an express prohibition against discrimination, arbitrators have "the power and responsibility" to enforce substantive human rights (and obligations) as if they were part of the collective agreement.

As a result, it may not longer be necessary, as a matter of law, to include a non-discrimination clause in a collective agreement in order for an arbitrator to have jurisdiction over a grievor's human rights allegations. Nonetheless, if the collective agreement does contain such a provision, it will further affirm the workplace parties' *Human Rights Code* obligations and bolster the argument that an arbitrator — as opposed to the Human Rights Tribunal — should adjudicate any alleged human rights contraventions that cannot be resolved by the parties.

Notably, the *Human Rights Code* only allows for the early dismissal of a human rights application where another proceeding has, in whole or in part, appropriately dealt with the substance of the application; the fact that an arbitrator may have the jurisdiction to deal with the substance of the allegations is an insufficient basis for dismissal. Furthermore, even if an arbitrator ultimately rejects a grievor's human rights allegations at arbitration, this does not preclude the grievor from filing a human rights complaint with the Human Rights Tribunal in an attempt to relitigate the matter in that forum. If this happens, the employer's recourse is to argue that the arbitrator appropriately dealt with the substance of the application and/or the *Human Rights Code*'s limitation period has passed (there is a one-year time limit for bringing an application) and/or the doctrine of *res judicata* or issue estoppel (as discussed above) applies because the matter has already been determined by a competent board of arbitration.

h) — Deemed termination

In addition to the collective agreement's "just cause" provision, some employers and unions have negotiated and agreed to "deemed termination" provisions that automatically terminate an employee's employment in certain prescribed circumstances. More specifically, the collective agreement may stipulate that an employee is deemed to be terminated from his or her employment if the employee is continuously absent for a given period of time (e.g. for a period of six months). The parties may have agreed to such a provision to eliminate the uncertainty associated with an indefinite period of employee absence due to sickness or injury.

For the most part, arbitrators and the courts have held that deemed termination provisions are unenforceable as they are discriminatory and contrary to human rights legislation. These clauses have been found to be discriminatory on the basis that an employee with an extended sickness or injury should have the same right as other employees to challenge his or her termination pursuant to the standard of just cause (i.e. his or her termination should not simply be "automatic" because a prescribed time period has passed). They have also been found to breach human rights legislation on the basis that the employer must be able to establish that it has accommodated the employee to the point of undue hardship in all cases.

However, on January 26, 2007, the Supreme Court of Canada issued a significant decision considering whether including automatic termination clauses in collective agreements is discriminatory and contrary to human rights legislation. In *Syndicat des employés de l'Hôpital général de Montréal c. Sexton*, [2007] 1 S.C.R. 161, 277 D.L.R. (4th) 577, 2007 CarswellQue 111, 2007 CarswellQue 110 (S.C.C.) (the "*McGill*" decision), the majority of the Supreme Court of Canada held that automatic termination clauses are *prima facie* discriminatory. However, an automatic termination clause is a form of "negotiated accommodation". Accordingly, the length of absence specified in an automatic termination clause, while not determinative, is a factor to consider when assessing the scope and limits of the duty to accommodate. In addition, the personal circumstances of the employee must be considered.

As a result, an employer should not terminate an employee's employment solely on the basis of a deemed termination provision. Rather, termination should be asserted both on the basis of the deemed termination clause in the collective agreement *and* on the basis of just cause in all of the circumstances. Employers should always proceed with caution when discharging employees, particularly if the employer seeks to rely on an automatic termination clause as the basis for the discharge. In every case, employers should consider the following principles that may be gleaned from the decision in *McGill*:

- There is value in negotiating specific termination clauses in connection with disability-related absenteeism.
- The content of specific termination clauses is indicative of how the parties have agreed to balance workplace interests and define the employer's approach to accommodation.
- The period of absence allowable under a specific termination clause is one of several factors relevant to the question of whether the employer has discharged its duty to accommodate in any given case.
- A clause that permits a lengthy period of absence is likely to meet the accommodation needs of many employees and will be more likely to withstand scrutiny.
- Regardless of the period of absence specified in an automatic termination clause, it remains necessary to assess, in each case, whether the duty to accommodate has been satisfied.

- The application of an automatic termination clause in circumstances where medical information suggests that the employee is expected to recover and return to work within a reasonable period of time is unlikely to be upheld by an arbitrator or court.

Significant Case Law

***Syndicat des employés de l'Hôpital général de Montréal c. Sexton*, [2007] 1 S.C.R. 161, 277 D.L.R. (4th) 577, 2007 CarswellQue 111, 2007 CarswellQue 110 (S.C.C.) (the "*McGill*" decision)**

The Supreme Court of Canada confirmed that if an employer takes an employee's personal circumstances and individual accommodation needs into account, and otherwise meets its duty to accommodate, the application of an automatic termination provision will not be discriminatory.

The Facts

In March, 2000, the employee took a leave of absence due to various problems with her health. The employer extended the six-month rehabilitation period set out in the collective agreement following negotiations with the union. Despite repeated attempts, the employer's efforts to assist the employee to return to work were unsuccessful.

The collective agreement included an automatic termination clause, which expressly provided that employees would lose their seniority rights and their employment after a thirty-six month of absence by reason of an illness or an accident other than an industrial accident or occupational disease. Pursuant to this clause, the employer notified the employee that her employment would terminate effective April 3, 2003. The employee failed to return to work by that date and, accordingly, the employer notified the employee that her employment had been automatically terminated. The union challenged the termination, alleging that the employer had failed to accommodate the employee's disability.

The Arbitrator dismissed the union's grievance. The Arbitrator found that the employer accommodated the employee by extending the prescribed rehabilitation period in the collective agreement. The Arbitrator also noted that the employee remained unfit for work at the end of the three-year period stipulated in the collective agreement. The Québec Superior Court of Justice upheld the Arbitrator's decision, but the Court of Appeal disagreed and the Arbitrator's decision was overturned. The employer appealed to the Supreme Court of Canada.

Before the Supreme Court, the employer argued that it had discharged its duty to accommodate the employee, particularly in view of the fact that the employee remained unable to return to work in the foreseeable future. The union argued that it was contradictory to argue that accommodation must be assessed on a case-by-case basis while allowing an employer to discharge its duty to accommodate by mechanically applying an automatic termination clause. Essentially, the union took the position that the automatic termination clause could not apply "automatically". The union argued that a careful consideration of the employee's individual circumstances was necessary before the employer could rely on the automatic termination clause to discharge the employee.

The Decision

The Supreme Court of Canada was divided 6 - 3 on the issue. Writing for the majority of the Court, Justice Deschamps held that automatic termination clauses are *prima facie* discriminatory. However, parties to a collective agreement have a right to negotiate, in good faith, provisions to ensure that employees attend and complete their work. The majority of the Court found that an automatic termination clause, while aimed at ill or disabled employees, is a form of "negotiated accommodation" freely bargained by the parties.

The majority of the Court found that the length of absence specified in an automatic termination clause is not determinative of the accommodation to which the employee is entitled. The specified length of absence is merely one factor to consider when assessing the scope and limits of the duty to accommodate. The majority of the Court emphasized that the right to equality is a fundamental right, meaning that parties to a collective agreement cannot negotiate a level of protection inferior to that afforded to employees pursuant to human rights legislation. As a result, employers and unions cannot definitively determine the applicable period in advance. The particular circumstances of each case must be weighed in conjunction with any automatic termination provision. The Court commented on the importance of taking an employee's individual accommodation needs into account at paragraph 22:

> The importance of the individualized nature of the accommodation process cannot be minimized. The scope of the duty to accommodate varies according to the characteristics of each enterprise, the specific needs of each employee and the specific circumstances in which the decision is to be made. Throughout the employment relationship, the employer must make an effort to accommodate the employee ... The obligation of the employer, the union and the employee is to come to a reasonable compromise. Reasonable accommodation is thus incompatible with the mechanical application of a general standard. In this sense, the Union is correct in saying that

the accommodation measure cannot be decided on by blindly applying a clause of the collective agreement.

The majority of the Court concluded that an automatic termination clause can be applied only if it is adapted to the individual circumstances of the specific case.

Applying its legal analysis to the facts, the majority of the Court found that the Arbitrator properly recognized that the employer did not apply the automatic termination clause in the collective agreement automatically. The Arbitrator correctly considered the particular facts and circumstances of the case, including all of the employer's efforts to accommodate the employee and the fact that the employee remained unable to return to work in the foreseeable future. In this context, the majority of the Court found that the Arbitrator was correct in concluding that the employer was not required to continue to employ the employee. As a consequence, in the particular circumstances of the case, the automatic termination provision in the collective agreement was not discriminatory.

The Implications

The *McGill* decision upholds the argument espoused by unions that automatic termination clauses cannot be applied "automatically" without consideration of the disabled employee's individual needs and the employer's ability to accommodate same. However, the decision balances the requirement to take an "individualized" approached against the finding that negotiated automatic termination clauses are not necessarily discriminatory and may be a significant factor in assessing whether the employer has met its duty to accommodate in any given case. The balance struck by the Court underscores the importance of the employer's duty to accommodate but also maintains the Court's traditional view that parties should be permitted to negotiate freely and enter into contracts with one another as they see fit.

Chapter 9: Potential Damages Arising from the Termination of Employment

9.1 — Overview

When deciding to dismiss an employee, employers must consider the financial implications that may arise, including the potential damages that may be awarded to the employee. Different considerations arise depending on whether the workplace is unionized.

If an employer discharges a unionized employee and fails to establish just cause at arbitration, the arbitrator will generally reinstate the employee with or without damages for lost wages.

A non-unionized employee who is found to have been dismissed without just cause will generally be entitled to damages based on the requirements of the *Employment Standards Act, 2000*, the express terms of any written contract of employment, and the common law. A non-unionized employee may elect to file a claim pursuant to the *Employment Standards Act, 2000* or commence a civil action for wrongful termination in the courts pursuant to the common law. An *Employment Standards Act, 2000* claim may result in the employee being awarded his or her statutory entitlements to termination and severance pay. Reinstatement may also be available in some cases of discharge contrary to the *Employment Standards Act, 2000*. If the employee elects to proceed in court, as opposed to filing an employment standards claim, the court will determine what the employee would have received had he or she been lawfully discharged in accordance with the employment contract and the common law. If the court finds that the employee was discharged without just cause or reasonable notice, it will then award damages for the employer's failure to give reasonable notice of termination of employment (or compensation in lieu of such notice).

9.2 — Unionized Employees

If an employer fails to establish just cause for discipline, an arbitrator may rescind the discipline. If, however, there is cause for discipline, the arbitrator will consider whether the penalty imposed by the employer was justified. Where the arbitrator finds that it is just and reasonable to do so, he or she may substitute a lesser penalty. For example, an arbitrator may substitute a suspension for a discharge. In determining the appropriate penalty, the arbitrator will consider mitigating factors such as the employee's length of service and disciplinary record.

In the case of a discharge without just cause, an arbitrator will typically reinstate the employee with compensation. The compensation awarded represents the employee's lost wages and may include such things as lost overtime and lost bonuses. In some cases, where the arbitrator finds that the employee committed some wrongdoing but that discharge is not justified, the arbitrator may reinstate the employee without compensation or with reduced compensation. In "exceptional" or "extraordinary" circumstances, arbitrators also have the jurisdiction to substitute an award of damages in lieu of reinstatement where the employee's discharge is not justified, but where the mutual mistrust between the employee and the employer is so pervasive that the employment relationship is untenable.

An employee has a duty to take reasonable steps to mitigate his or her damages. Accordingly, an employee who is discharged must make every best effort to find alternate employment as soon as possible. However, he or she is not required to actually find another job. Rather, reasonable efforts will suffice. Furthermore, it is not necessary for an employee to accept any offer of employment. It is reasonable for an employee to decline an employment offer for work that is significantly inferior or otherwise not "comparable" to his or her previous position.

If the employee fails to make reasonable efforts to find alternative employment, an arbitrator may reduce the compensation that otherwise would have been awarded to the employee. However, if he or she does find alternative employment, his or her earnings from the subsequent employment may be deducted from the compensation awarded.

9.3 — Non-Unionized Employees

a) — The *Employment Standards Act, 2000*

The *Employment Standards Act, 2000* sets out an employer's minimum statutory obligations. The *Employment Standards Act, 2000* provides for both notice of termination, or pay in lieu thereof, and severance pay, subject to various prescribed exemptions. Accordingly, if an employee is discharged, he or she may file an employment standards claim seeking statutory termination and severance pay. There are numerous exemptions to the provisions for termination and severance pay. However, the one most commonly relied upon in cases of employee misconduct giving rise to discharge is the exemption for an employee who is guilty of wilful misconduct, disobedience or wilful neglect of duty that is not trivial and has not been condoned by the employer. Unless the employer can establish that the employee falls within that or another exemption, an order may be issued requiring the employer to pay termination and severance pay.

i) — Notice of termination/termination pay

The minimum statutory notice period ranges from one week for employees whose period of employment is less than one year to eight weeks for employees whose period of employment is eight years or more. No notice is required for employees who have been employed for less than three months. The statutory notice periods are set out in the following chart:

Length of Service	Notice
Less than 3 months	Nil
3 months but less than 1 year	1 week
1 year but less than 3 years	2 weeks
3 years but less than 4 years	3 weeks
4 years but less than 5 years	4 weeks
5 years but less than 6 years	5 weeks
6 years but less than 7 years	6 weeks
7 years but less than 8 years	7 weeks
8 years or more	8 weeks

The notice of termination may be actual notice wherein the employee remains at work during the notice period or it may be provided by way of pay in lieu of notice, which is referred to as "termination pay". Statutory termination pay is equal to the amount of wages that the employee would have been entitled to receive during the prescribed notice period calculated at his or her regular rate for a regular non-overtime work week. In addition, during the notice period, the employer must continue to provide standard benefits and contribute to the pension plan.

Notice of termination is not required in all circumstances. As set out above, an employee is not entitled to notice of termination if he or she is guilty of wilful misconduct, disobedience or wilful neglect of duty that is not trivial and has not been condoned by the employer. Similarly, an employee who is discharged after refusing an offer of reasonable alternative employment with the employer is not entitled to notice of termination. Other exceptions from the termination provisions are set out in the *Employment Standards Act, 2000* and its regulations.

Special provisions apply if the employer terminates the employment of 50 or more employees in the same four-week period. Such a situation is referred to as a "mass termination". When a mass termination takes place, the employer must provide certain prescribed information to the Director of Employment Standards and follow other procedures set out in the *Employment Standards Act, 2000* and its regulations. Employees subject to a mass termination have enhanced notice entitlements, notwithstanding any individual employee's length of service. The statutory notice period applicable in a mass termination depends on the number of employees being dismissed, and ranges from eight to 16 weeks.

ii) — Severance pay

In *addition* to statutory termination pay, the *Employment Standards Act, 2000* requires that statutory severance pay be paid to an employee who has at least five years of service and who is one of 50 or more employees to have their employment severed in a six-month period because all or part of the business closed at an establishment. An employee with at least five years of service is also entitled to severance pay if his or her employer has an annual payroll of at least

$2.5 million. An employer's payroll will be considered to be at least $2.5 million if either:

- the total wages earned by all of the employer's employees in the four weeks that end with the last day of the last pay period completed prior to the severance of an employee's employment is $2.5 million or more when multiplied by 13; or
- the total wages earned by all of the employer's employees in the last or second-last fiscal year of the employer prior to the severance of an employee's employment was $2.5 million or more.

Employers should note that the payrolls of associated or related corporations may be treated as one for the purpose of determining whether an employer has a payroll of $2.5 million. It should also be noted that the Employment Standards Practices Branch (the "Branch") only considers wages paid to employees in Ontario, and not those in other jurisdictions, when calculating an employer's payroll.

The severance pay obligation is in addition to any notice or termination pay requirements under the *Employment Standards Act, 2000* and cannot be reduced by giving more notice of termination than the minimum required by the *Employment Standards Act, 2000*. Unlike termination pay, severance pay cannot be "worked off". However, severance pay can be paid in instalments with the employee's written agreement.

The *Employment Standards Act, 2000* provides for exceptions to severance pay entitlements on the basis of the employee's conduct or the employment relationship. For example, as with termination pay, an employee is not entitled to severance pay if he or she is guilty of wilful misconduct, disobedience or wilful neglect of duty that is not trivial and has not been condoned by the employer. Other exemptions are set out in the *Employment Standards Act, 2000* and its regulations.

b) — The common law

As an alternative to filing an employment standards claim, a non-unionized employee who is discharged may commence a wrongful dismissal action in court pursuant to the common law. The common law entitles non-unionized employees to notice of termination. Specifically, in the absence of just cause or an express contractual limitation, a non-unionized employee who is dismissed is entitled to receive reasonable notice of the dismissal or pay in lieu thereof. If reasonable notice or pay in lieu thereof is not provided, the court will award the employee wrongful dismissal damages unless the employer can establish just cause for the employee's dismissal.

A court will determine damages based on the fundamental principle that a wronged employee is entitled to be put in as good a position as he or she would have been in if he or she had been given reasonable notice or pay in lieu thereof. Such damages may include the wages the employee would have earned and the cost of all benefits, pension and other entitlements the employee would have received if he or she had been given reasonable working notice of his or her termination of employment.

The amount of notice that is reasonable will vary from case to case, based on all the circumstances of the employment relationship. While there is no specific formula that can be applied uniformly to all cases, a court may consider the following factors when determining the reasonable notice period:

- the character of the employment;
- the employee's length of service;
- the age of the employee;
- the employee's salary level at and prior to termination;
- the availability of similar employment, having regard to the experience, training, and qualifications of the employee;
- the employee's education;
- any inducement to leave a previous employer;
- the employee's history of advancement within the employer's organization;
- the economic circumstances facing both the employee and the employer; and
- the employee's degree of specialization.

A court will determine the reasonable notice period based on the particular circumstances of each case. Generally, courts have accepted that there is no minimum or maximum period of reasonable notice. While the case law indicates that there is no upper limit on the appropriate period of notice, notice in excess of 24 months is only warranted in exceptional cases. For example, in *Lowndes v. Summit Ford Sales Ltd.* (2006), 2006 CarswellOnt 11 (Ont. C.A.), additional reasons at (2006), 48 C.C.E.L. (3d) 194, 2006 CarswellOnt 2184 (Ont. C.A.), the Ontario Court of Appeal considered whether there is a "cap" on the amount of notice that is reasonable and stated:

> Although it is true that reasonable notice of employment termination must be determined on a case-specific basis and there is no absolute upper limit or cap on what constitutes reasonable notice, generally only exceptional circumstances will support a base notice period in excess of 24 months.

Notably, payments for termination or severance pay under the *Employment Standards Act, 2000* may be deducted from damages obtained by a plaintiff in a wrongful dismissal action.

Furthermore, non-unionized employees, like unionized employees, have a duty to mitigate their damages by seeking alternative employment.

i) — Bad faith discharge

Historically, any award of damages beyond compensation for breach of contract for failure to give reasonable notice of termination had to be based on an independent actionable wrong (e.g., defamation, intentional infliction of mental anguish, or assault). However, in *Wallace v. United Grain Growers Ltd.* (1997), 3 C.B.R. (4th) 1, 36 C.C.E.L. (2d) 1, [1997] 3 S.C.R. 701, 1997 CarswellMan 456, 1997 CarswellMan 455, 152 D.L.R. (4th) 1 (S.C.C.), the Supreme Court of Canada found that where the manner of dismissal does not constitute an independent actionable wrong, the employee is not without recourse. Rather, the Court had the discretion to extend the reasonable notice period to reflect the mental distress suffered as a result of the manner of dismissal. The Court found that an employer has an obligation to act in good faith and fairly deal with an employee in the manner by which it terminates the employment of an employee. More specifically, an employer is required to treat the employee in a candid, reasonable, honest, and forthright manner. The employer must refrain from engaging in any conduct that is unfair or in bad faith by being, for example, untruthful, misleading, or unduly insensitive. Similarly, the employer should not recklessly allege just cause for discharge in the absence of a reasonable basis for the allegation.

Any bad faith conduct in the manner of dismissal may be compensated by a court by an *increase* to the period of reasonable notice. As not all acts of bad faith or unfair dealing are equally injurious to an employee, the amount by which the notice period was to be extended due to such acts was to vary depending on the circumstances.

Following the issuance of the Supreme Court of Canada's decision in *Wallace*, claims for "*Wallace* damages" became routine in wrongful dismissal litigation. Despite some judicial criticism regarding plaintiffs advancing clearly unmeritorious *Wallace* claims, these claims frequently served to prolong litigation and increase the parties' costs as well as increasing potential liability for employers.

Ultimately, the Supreme Court of Canada reformulated the manner and circumstances in which damages for bad faith in the manner of dismissal may be awarded. Specifically, in *Keays v. Honda Canada Inc.*, 2008 CarswellOnt 3743, 2008 CarswellOnt 3744, 294 D.L.R. (4th) 577, [2008] 2 S.C.R. 362 (S.C.C.), the Supreme Court rejected the approach of arbitrarily increasing the notice period to compensate for bad faith or unfair dealing in the manner of dismissal. Rather, the Court found that if an employee can prove that the manner of dismissal caused mental distress that was in the contemplation of the parties, mental distress damages may be awarded to the extent that actual damages are established by the employee. The Court emphasized that damages for bad faith at the time of termination must be limited to compensatory damages. The Court stated that examples of conduct in dismissal resulting in compensable damages are "attacking the employee's reputation by declaration made at the time of dismissal, misrepresentation regarding the reason for the decision, or dismissal meant to deprive the employee of a pension benefit or other right".

In short, based on the *Keays* decision, an employee claim for damages for bad faith dismissal should be adjudicated based upon the following principles:

- Such damages are available only where the employer engaged in conduct during the course of dismissal that was unfair or was in bad faith;
- Such an award must be limited to compensatory damages and not be punitive;

- In order to be entitled to damages for bad faith, a plaintiff must demonstrate that mental distress damages were in the contemplation of the parties; and
- Such damages should not be awarded through an arbitrary extension of the notice period. Rather, an award should reflect the actual damages that resulted from the employer's conduct.

c) — Damages for loss of benefits during the period of reasonable notice

Non-unionized employees are entitled to receive damages for loss of the benefits they would have enjoyed had they been provided with reasonable working notice of termination. Therefore, in addition to damages that may be awarded based on the employee's salary, an employer may be liable for damages with respect to any lost benefits including pension and any "out of pocket" expenses incurred in obtaining replacement employment.

i) — Vacation pay

One issue that frequently arises when calculating damages for lost benefits concerns entitlement to vacation pay. A wrongfully dismissed employee is entitled to vacation pay during the statutory notice period pursuant to the *Employment Standards Act, 2000*. However, generally, no additional damages are payable in respect of vacation pay during the common law reasonable notice period in excess of the statutory minimum.

ii) — Pensions

The most commonly adopted formula for calculating pension loss is the "commuted value methodology". This method determines the difference between the commuted present value of the employee's pension benefits at the time of discharge and its commuted present value at the date corresponding with the end of the period of reasonable notice. The difference between these two figures represents the pension loss suffered by the employee. Typically, the plan administrator and actuaries will become involved in this calculation.

iii) — Group benefit plans

Pursuant to the *Employment Standards Act, 2000*, employees are entitled to continued benefit coverage during the statutory notice period. An employer is required to continue to make whatever benefit plan contributions are necessary to maintain the employee's benefits until the end of the statutory notice period. Even if the employer discharges the employee with pay in lieu of notice, the employer must continue to make whatever benefit plan contributions are required to maintain the benefits the employee would have received had he or she continued to be employed during the statutory notice period. If an employer fails to contribute to a benefit plan, the amount the employer should have contributed shall be deemed to be unpaid wages owing to the employee and the employer may be liable for benefits as if it were the insurer. In most cases, insurers will provide coverage during the statutory period based on the common law principle that a contract of insurance must be read in conformity with statutory law.

With respect to the common law reasonable notice period, it is well established that employers may face liability for failing to provide dismissed employees with disability benefits during this period.

It is an implied term in the employment contract that benefit coverage will continue throughout the common law notice period based on the principle that the employee should be placed in the same position as he or she would have been in had the employer not breached the contract. If benefit coverage is discontinued and the employee becomes disabled during the reasonable notice period at common law, the employer may be liable for the benefits the employee would have received had his or her insurance been continued. An employer that does not or is unable to continue group benefit coverage during the period of reasonable notice is necessarily running the risk of being held liable for damages flowing from the loss of such benefit coverage.

The most recent statement on the issue of disability claims during the reasonable notice period is *Egan v. Alcatel Canada Inc.* (2006), 2006 CarswellOnt 28, 47 C.C.E.L. (3d) 87 (Ont. C.A.), leave to appeal refused (2006), 2006 CarswellOnt 4796, 2006 CarswellOnt 4795, 225 O.A.C. 398 (note) (S.C.C.). Alcatel was only prepared to maintain Egan's group insurance benefits over the notice period mandated by the *Employment Standards Act, 2000* or until September 25, 2002. Within three months of her termination, and during her attempt to find work, Egan became disabled on October 1, 2002. Egan remained disabled for one year. The Court of Appeal found that the trial judge was correct in his determination that the reasonable notice period was nine months. On the issue of lost disability benefits, the Court of Appeal stated, at paragraph 26:

> Where an employee would otherwise have qualified for disability benefits during the reasonable notice period, but the application is denied on the basis that coverage was wrongfully discontinued by the employer, the employer must be liable for the value of the disability benefits that would otherwise have been payable. Ms Egan was entitled to the continuation of all forms of compensation, including employee benefits, during the reasonable notice period.

The Court of Appeal upheld the trial judge's award of full salary for the notice period prior to the onset of disability. However, the Court withdrew the trial judge's award of full salary for the six-month period during which Egan's disability and reasonable notice period overlapped. Instead, the Court of Appeal provided Egan with disability benefits for the duration of her disability — which amounted to twelve months.

Some employers offer to pay employees the value of the employer's share of premiums for the notice period. However, in the absence of a signed severance agreement and release, a court may not necessarily find payment of the employer's premium costs to be an adequate quantification of the damages suffered by the employee.

Where an employee is entitled to receive disability benefits or would have been entitled to receive them but for the employer's failure to continue coverage, the next issue to be considered is the interaction between disability payments and payments in lieu of notice of termination. During the statutory notice and severance periods, based on the language of the *Employment Standards Act, 2000*, there is a strong argument that disability benefits cannot be set off against termination or severance pay. The common law rules are set out in a series of cases reviewed below.

In *Sylvester v. British Columbia*, 146 D.L.R. (4th) 207, 1997 CarswellBC 1024, 1997 CarswellBC 1025, [1997] 2 S.C.R. 315 (S.C.C.), the Supreme Court of Canada set out guidelines regarding when disability payments should be deducted from pay in lieu of notice. The Court stated that deductibility "depends on the intention of the parties to the employment contract" and whether the disability plans should be considered to be distinct from the employment contract or integral components of it. The Court examined the terms of the employment contract and the disability plans in question and concluded that the disability contracts were integral components of the employment contract for two reasons. First, the terms of the disability plans demonstrated that the disability benefits were intended to be a substitute for the employee's regular salary. Second, the simultaneous payment of disability benefits and damages for wrongful dismissal was inconsistent with the employment contract. This inconsistency arose because wrongful dismissal damages are based on the premise that the employee would have worked during the notice period and disability benefits are based on the premise that the employee is unable to work. The Court stated:

> It makes no sense to pay damages based on the assumption that he would have worked in addition to disability benefits which arose solely because he could not work. This suggests that the parties did not intend the respondent to receive both damages and disability benefits.

In the circumstances, the Court concluded that disability benefits should be deducted from the award of damages. However, the Court noted two "exceptions" to its approach. First, where the parties agree, the employee may receive both disability benefits and damages for wrongful dismissal. The Court stated that such an agreement or "intention" could be inferred if it was not expressly indicated in the contract. Second, the employee may receive both disability benefits and damages for wrongful dismissal where the "benefits are akin to benefits from a private insurance plan for which the employee has provided consideration". Notably, in the case before the Court, the employee did not make any contributions to the disability plan.

These exceptions have been interpreted very broadly by the Ontario Court of Appeal: *Sills v. Children's Aid Society of Belleville (City), Hastings (County) & Trenton (City)* (2001), 198 D.L.R. (4th) 485, 53 O.R. (3d) 577, 2001 CarswellOnt 1448 (Ont. C.A.), and *McNamara v. Alexander Centre Industries Ltd.* (2001), 199 D.L.R. (4th) 717, 53 O.R. (3d) 481, 2001 CarswellOnt 1441 (Ont. C.A.), leave to appeal refused (2001), 2001 CarswellOnt 3808, 2001 CarswellOnt 3807, 158 O.A.C. 195 (note) (S.C.C.). In both of these decisions, the Court held that the employees were entitled to receive both disability benefits and pay in lieu of notice during the relevant notice period.

In *Sills*, the employer received an employment insurance premium reduction for having its disability plan. Instead of remitting that reduction to employees, the employer redirected it to the benefit premiums. Accordingly, employees nominally and indirectly contributed to the costs of the insurance plan. Furthermore, the trial judge found that Sills earned the disability benefits "as part of her compensation and as part of a trade-off in arriving at benefits and salary". The Court concluded that it was reasonable to infer that the parties would agree that an employee could retain disability benefits in addition to damages for wrongful dismissal. Specifically, the Court stated:

> I consider it reasonable to assume that an employee would not willingly negotiate and pay for a benefit that would allow her employer to avoid responsibility for a wrongful act. I consider it reasonable to infer that the parties would agree that an employee should retain disability benefits in addition to damages for wrongful dismissal where the employee has effectively paid for the benefits in question.

Accordingly, the Court found that disability benefits should not be deducted from wrongful dismissal damages.

In *McNamara*, the employee made no direct payments for the benefits as his employer paid the full premium. However, the employee testified that he would not have accepted his salary but for the benefit package. This was accepted as evidence that there had been some consideration in return for the provision of benefits. The Court also distinguished *Sylvester* on the basis that the benefits were paid directly to the employee from a third party, in this case, London Life. Based on these factors, the Court inferred that the parties would have intended for the employee to receive both disability benefits and damages for wrongful dismissal.

It should be noted that in some jurisdictions, *Sylvester* has not been so narrowly construed. However, at least in Ontario, disability benefits are unlikely to be deducted from wrongful dismissal damages if there is any evidence that the employee contributed to the cost of the benefits, either directly or indirectly.

It is difficult to reconcile *Egan* with the *Sylvester* line of cases. Specifically, applying *Sylvester* to the facts in *Egan*, it would appear that *Egan* should have been entitled to receive full pay in lieu of notice for the entire notice period. The issue of whether disability benefits should be received in addition to notice pay or should be set off against notice pay would be based upon whether the employee contributed to disability benefits (e.g. through premiums or otherwise). However, as set out above, in *Egan*, the Court awarded full pay only until the onset of disability and disability benefits thereafter. It could, therefore, be argued that the employee never received full compensation for the entire notice period. This apparent inconsistency and its significance will, no doubt, be the subject of further litigation. While *Egan* "muddied the waters" regarding the issue of set off, it does clearly stand for the proposition that an employee may be entitled to disability benefits for the duration of a disability notwithstanding that the disability extends beyond the end of the reasonable notice period.

9.4 — Aggravated and Punitive Damages

a) — The Law Following *Wallace*

Following the Supreme Court of Canada's 1997 decision in *Wallace v. United Grain Growers Ltd.* (1997), 3 C.B.R. (4th) 1, [1997] 3 S.C.R. 701, 1997 CarswellMan 456, 1997 CarswellMan 455, 152 D.L.R. (4th) 1 (S.C.C.), both aggravated and punitive damages were awarded only in the narrowest of circumstances, having regard to established caselaw from the courts. Generally speaking, aggravated damages can be defined as damages that are intended to compensate an employee for intangible and non-pecuniary losses. Damages for mental distress or hurt feelings would be examples. Conversely, punitive damages are non-compensatory and are awarded where the court wishes to punish the employer for particularly offensive or egregious behaviour and deter other employers from engaging in similar behaviour. In the unionized context, the issue of whether an arbitrator has the jurisdiction to award aggravated or punitive damages continues to be a matter of debate.

As stated above, the Supreme Court of Canada in *Wallace* indicated that both aggravated and punitive damages should be awarded only in the narrowest of circumstances. In fact, the employer must be found to have committed an independent actionable wrong during or in connection with the employee's dismissal. Typically, this independent actionable wrong would be founded upon some sort of tortious action. A tort is a civil wrong. Examples would include the tort of intentional infliction of mental suffering or the tort of defamation. Essentially, the reason the Supreme Court of Canada required that an employee establish an independent actionable wrong in order to claim aggravated or punitive damages is because the employment relationship is contractual in nature. That is, because the parties to an employment contract are deemed to have contemplated that the employment relationship can be terminated, the fact of termination of the employment contract should not normally give rise to more than an entitlement to reasonable notice.

Examples of behaviours that have been found by courts to justify an award for aggravated and punitive damages include:

- baseless allegations of serious misconduct such as dishonesty or gross incompetence;
- a failure to properly investigate alleged misconduct and to give the employee an opportunity to respond to the employer's findings; and
- harassment, intimidation, or humiliation of the employee.

For a further discussion of the Supreme Court of Canada decision in *Wallace*, see the Bad Faith Discharge section of Chapter 9.3, above.

b) — The Law Following *Keays*

In 2008, the Supreme Court of Canada released its decision in *Honda Canada Inc. v. Keays*, [2008] S.C.J. 40. With this decision, the Supreme Court of Canada has reformulated the law of damages in wrongful dismissal. The three most important principles which emerge from the *Keays* decision are as follows.

First, there is no longer a distinction between so-called "*Wallace*" damages (which resulted in an increase in the reasonable notice period entitlement) and "aggravated" damages (which required an independent actionable wrong). Rather, the question in every case is what damages are reasonably foreseeable and deemed to be within the contemplation of the parties as a result of the breach of the employment contract.

Second, in addition to receiving reasonable notice (subject to the express terms of a legally enforceable employment contract), an employee can receive compensatory damages for conduct in the manner of dismissal if, but only if, that manner of dismissal actually results in provable mental distress or other damages being suffered by the employee. If such is the case, then the damages awarded will be proportionate to the injuries suffered by the employee. In other words, employers are still subject to the *Wallace* concept of acting in good faith in the manner of dismissal. But if an employer breaches that duty of good faith in the manner of dismissal, the employee is not automatically entitled to a bump up in the period of reasonable notice. In the wake of *Wallace*, employees often received a bump up in the period of reasonable notice even without any evidence that the employee was directly affected by the employer's breach of good faith. Following the Supreme Court of Canada's decision in *Keays*, if the employer acts in bad faith, the employee will have to prove that this has resulted in actual mental distress and the damages will be quantified accordingly.

Third, non-compensatory punitive damages should be restricted to advertent (as opposed to inadvertent) wrongful acts that are so malicious and outrageous that they are deserving of punishment by the court for the purposes of deterrence. Further, courts should resort to punitive damages only in the most exceptional of cases and, even then, only where the court is of the view that the compensatory damages awarded are not adequate enough to bring home to the employer that its conduct was inappropriate.

More specifically, the Supreme Court of Canada held that there are two requirements for awarding punitive damages: first, there must be an independent actionable wrong; and second, the conduct meriting punitive damages must be "harsh, vindictive, reprehensible and malicious", as well as "extreme in its nature and such that by any reasonable standard it is deserving of full condemnation and punishment".

In *Keays*, the Supreme Court of Canada found that the lower Courts' award of punitive damages (which amounted to $500,000 at trial, but which was reduced to $100,000 by the Ontario Court of Appeal) was based on Honda's discriminatory conduct and resulting breach of the Ontario *Human Rights Code*. The Court of Appeal had also relied on Honda's refusal to deal with Keays's counsel as part of its reasons for justifying an award of punitive damages. The Supreme Court of Canada found, however, that Honda's conduct was not sufficiently egregious or outrageous to warrant rebuke from the courts. As a result, the $100,000 in punitive damages awarded to the plaintiff was set aside. Further, as long as an employee and employer are in an employment relationship, the "parties are always entitled to deal with each other directly" and that there was no obligation on the part of Honda to deal with Keays's counsel.

Finally, in *Keays*, the Supreme Court of Canada addressed whether Honda's discriminatory conduct could amount to an "independent actionable wrong" for the purposes of awarding punitive damages. On balance, this decision appears to suggest that even if Honda's conduct did amount to discriminatory behaviour under the *Code*, based on previous law, a breach of the *Code* cannot amount to an independent actionable wrong on which an award of punitive damages can be based.

Index

A

Absenteeism, *see also* Employee conduct, specific types of
- culpable absenteeism, 69-72
- • attendance management program, unilaterally imposed, 71-72
- • attendance management program, validity of, 72
- • inclement weather, 70-71
- • misconduct, form of, 69-70
- employment standards leaves, 73
- • *Employment Standards Act, 2000*, compliance with, 73
- • "non-monitored" absences, 73
- innocent absenteeism, 64-69
- • common law doctrine of "frustration", 65-66
- • • factors considered, 66
- • disability, underlying, 66
- • dismissal, procedural requirements for, 65
- • employment relationship impaired, 64-65
- • excessive absenteeism, 64-65
- • frustration of contract by disability, 66-69
- • • amendment to ESA regulation, 69
- • • "deemed terminated", 67, 68-69
- • • statutory severance pay, entitlement to, 66-69
- • incapable of regular attendance, 65
- • innocent vs. culpable absenteeism, 64

C

Collective agreement clauses, *see also* Unionized employees
- introduction, 109
- sample clauses, 109-118
- • deemed termination, 114-118
- • • "negotiated accommodation", 115
- • • personal circumstances and individual accommodation to be considered, 116-118
- • • principles gleaned from *McGill* decision, 115-116

Collective agreement clauses *(cont'd)*
• • • whether discriminatory and contrary to human rights legislation, 114-118
• • just cause, 109
• • non-discrimination clause, 113-114
• • • affirming workplace parties' *Human Rights Code* obligations, 113-114
• • personnel files, reviewing, 111-112
• • reasons, issuing, 111
• • sunset clauses, 112-113
• • • examples, 112
• • • progressive discipline more difficult, 113
• • timeliness, 110
• • union representative, presence of, 110-111

Constructive discipline
• generally, v
• non-unionized workplace, 2-3

D

Damages arising from termination of employment
• aggravated and punitive damages, 132-135
• • examples of behaviours justifying, 133
• • law following *Keays*, 133-135
• • • compensatory damages for provable mental distress, 133-134
• • • foreseeability of damages, 133
• • • non-compensatory punitive damages, 134
• non-unionized employees, 121-132
• • common law, 123-125
• • • bad faith discharge, 125-127
• • • • mental distress damages, 126-127
• • • • "*Wallace* damages", 125-126
• • • reasonable notice period, factors determining, 124-125
• • *Employment Standards Act, 2000*, 121-123
• • • notice of termination, 121-122
• • • severance pay, 122-123
• • • statutory notice periods, 121-122
• • • termination pay, 121-122
• • • where fifty or more employees, 122
• • loss of benefits during period of reasonable notice, 127-132
• • • group benefit plans, 128-132

Damages arising from termination of employment *(cont'd)*
• • • • disability claims during reasonable notice period, 128-129
• • • • disability payments vs. payments in lieu of notice, 129-132
• • • • implied term that coverage continuing throughout common law period, 128
• • • pensions, 127
• • • vacation pay, 127
• overview, 119
• unionized employees, 120
• • arbitrator's discretion, 120
• • discharge without just cause, 120
• • • reinstatement with compensation, 120
• • • • damages in lieu of reinstatement, 120
• • employee's duty to mitigate, 120

Disciplinary investigation
• introduction, 9
• necessary information, obtaining, 11-12
• purposes of investigation, 9-10
• • five important purposes, 9-10
• • relevant records or reports, creating or gathering, 10
• report, investigation, 15-17
• • sample outline of disciplinary investigation report, 15-17
• timing of investigation, 10-11
• witnesses, interviewing, 12-15
• • final witness being person who was subject of discipline, 13
• • keys to effective interview, 13-15
• • witnesses with any degree of involvement, 12

Disciplinary letter, elements of, *see also* Disciplinary letters, sample
• disciplinary penalty being applied, 81-82
• disciplinary record, 81
• employee support: positive aspect of disciplinary penalty, 82
• infraction, 81
• introduction, 81
• notice of future discipline, serving, 82
• sample disciplinary letter, 82-83

Disciplinary letters, sample
• introduction, 85
• sample letters, 85-89
• • dismissal for damaging company property, 88
• • suspension for fighting, 85-86

Disciplinary letters,
sample *(cont'd)*
• • suspension for theft, 87-88
• • suspension for unauthorized absence from work, 86-87
• • warning for failure to adhere to safety policies, 88-89
• • warning for unauthorized absence from work, 86

Disciplinary meeting
• after dismissal, 97-106
• • other employees, 98
• • personal items, 97
• • post-discharge obligations, 98-106
• • • "fair competition", 98
• • • fiduciary employees, 99-101, 105-106
• • • • criteria for relationship, 99
• • • • fiduciary duties, 99-10067
• • • non-competition ban/non-solicitation agreement, 100-101
• • • non-fiduciary employees, 100-104
• • • • competing with former employer, 101-104
• • • • reasonable notice of resignation, 102, 103, 104
• • • proprietary confidential information, protection of, 98-99
• • • restrictive covenants , 104
• • references, 97-98
• • • employee having duty to mitigate, 97
• • • employer providing neutral and objective information, 98
• clarity and completeness, 92
• disciplinary records, maintaining, 106-108
• • *Employment Standards Act, 2000* requirements, 107
• • non-unionized employees, 107-108
• • • claim for damages for wrongful dismissal, 107-108
• • • • limitation period of two years, 107-108
• • unionized environment, 106-107
• • • grievance files, 106, 107
• • • *res judicata*, doctrine of, 106-107
• • • sunset clauses, 107
• following up after disciplinary meeting, 94
• introduction, 91
• location, 93
• resign, offer to, 93-94
• termination meeting, 95-96
• • checklist for conducting meeting, 95-96
• • • structure of meeting and confidentiality, 95
• timing, 93

Disciplinary meeting *(cont'd)*
• tone, 91-92
• witnesses, 92

Disciplinary penalty, selecting appropriate
• factors influencing discipline/discharge, 19-24
• • collective agreement or employment contract, 20
• • culminating incident, doctrine of, 22-23
• • explanation of employee, 23
• • offence, severity and nature of, 21
• • policies and procedures, applicable, 20-21
• • previous cases and consistency, 20-21
• • previous record of employee, 22-23
• • • elements of record to be considered, 22
• • • sunset clauses in collective agreements, 23
• • provocation, 23
• • relevant circumstances, additional, 23-24
• • • context of disciplinary response, 24
• • • personal circumstances, 23-24
• • • status of employee as union official, 24
• key factors considered, 19-20
• statutorily prohibited motives (Ontario legislation), 24-36
• • *Employment Standards Act, 2000*, 26-29
• • • discipline prohibited for exercising rights under ESA, 26-27
• • • order of employment standards officer, 27
• • • rights under ESA, 27
• • *Labour Relations Act, 1995*, 25-26
• • • complaint vs. civil proceedings, 29
• • • discipline not to be motivated by anti-union animus, 26
• • • • factors considered, 26
• • • non-unionized employees having right to file complaints, 28-29
• • • proceedings before OLRB, 25-26
• • • • remedial orders, 26
• • • unfair labour practices, 25
• • • unionized employees bound by decision of trade union, 27-28
• • • • subject to arbitration, 27-28
• • *Occupational Health and Safety Act*, 35
• • • complaint with OLRB, 35
• • • • where disciplined contrary to OHSA, 35
• • *Ontario Human Rights Code*, 30-34

Disciplinary penalty, selecting appropriate *(cont'd)*
- • • • applications and responses, 31
- • • • arbitrators in union setting having power to apply Code, 31-32
- • • • complaint where disciplined contrary to OHRC, 30
- • • • equal treatment, right to, 30
- • • • orders of Tribunal, 31
- • • • remedial powers of courts, 33-34
- • • • • non-monetary personal remedies, 34
- • • • • restitutive power, 33-34
- • • • time limit for filing complaint, 31
- • • • where prohibited from filing application, 34
- • • *Workplace Safety and Insurance Act, 1997*, 35-36

Disciplinary procedure
- • progressive discipline, 2-6
- • • disciplinary penalties involved in progressive discipline, 3-6
- • • • demotions, 5-6
- • • • dismissal, 6
- • • • suspensions without pay/final warnings, 4-5
- • • • verbal warnings, 3
- • • • written warnings, 4
- • • fundamental breach, 2-3
- • • non-unionized workplace, 2-3
- • • • constructive discipline, v, 2-3
- • • unionized workplace, 2
- • purposes of discipline, 1-2
- • • confidence and respect, 1
- • • deterrence, 1
- • • rehabilitation, 1
- • rehabilitation, opportunity for, 2
- • when to apply disciplinary procedure, 6-7
- • • poor performance addressed through "non-disciplinary" measures, 6-7

E

Emergency leave, *see Employment Standards Act, 2000*

Employee conduct, specific types of
- • absenteeism, 64-73
- • • culpable absenteeism, 69-72
- • • • attendance management program, unilaterally imposed, 71-72
- • • • attendance management program, validity of, 72
- • • • inclement weather, 70-71
- • • • misconduct, form of, 69-70
- • • employment standards leaves, 73

Employee conduct, specific types of *(cont'd)*
• • • *Employment Standards Act, 2000*, compliance with, 73
• • • "non-monitored" absences, 73
• • innocent absenteeism, 64-69
• • • common law doctrine of "frustration", 65-66
• • • • factors considered, 66
• • • disability, underlying, 66
• • • dismissal, procedural requirements for, 65
• • • employment relationship impaired, 64-65
• • • excessive absenteeism, 64-65
• • • frustration of contract by disability, 66-69
• • • • amendment to ESA regulation, 69
• • • • "deemed terminated", 67, 68-69
• • • • statutory severance pay, entitlement to, 66-69
• • • incapable of regular attendance, 65
• • • innocent vs. culpable absenteeism, 64
• company rules, breaching, 63-64
• conflict of interest, 57
• criminal convictions, 58-63
• • factors considered, 58
• • principles in assessing response to off-duty criminal charges, 62-63
• • significant case law: sexual assaulting minor, 61-62
• dishonesty, 42-48
• • breakdown of employment relationship, 43-48
• • • contextual approach, 47-48
• • • dishonesty about medical condition, 43-44
• • • exemplary performance record, 45, 46, 47
• • • *McKinley* test, 46
• • • nature and extent of misconduct, 46-47
• • • position of trust, 45, 47
• • mitigating factors, 42
• • when dishonesty constituting just cause for discharge, 30-31
• fighting/violence in workplace, 48-52
• • consultation paper, 48-49
• • • criminal victimization in workplace, 48-49
• • • reasonable precautions taken by employers, 49
• • • stakeholders providing input, 49
• • cost of workplace violence, 51
• • physically assaulting manager or supervisor, 51-52

Employee conduct, specific types of *(cont'd)*
• • proposed changes to OHSA, 49-51
• • • domestic violence, 50
• • • new work refusal procedures, 51
• • • risk of violence assessment, 50
• • • workplace violence programs, 50-51
• • • written policies, 49
• • significant case law, 52-54
• • • delay in imposing discipline, 52-54
• • • "stay of proceedings" not amounting to condonation, 52-53
• • • threatening conduct, 52, 53
• harassment, sexual and discriminatory, 55-57
• • *Human Rights Code*, prohibited by, 55
• • significant case law: after-hours conduct, 56-57
• • whether offending employee knew that conduct was unwelcome, 55
• insubordination, 54
• • unionized environment, 54
• • • "obey now — grieve later" principle and exceptions, 54
• introduction, 37
• last chance agreements (LCA), 76-80
• • accommodation, form of, 77
• • drafting considerations, 77-78
• • limiting arbitrator's jurisdiction, 76-77
• • significant case law: absenteeism due to alcohol abuse, 78-80
• • • "accommodation" under *Human Rights Act*, 78, 79
• • • appropriateness of LCA, 79-80
• lateness, 41-42
• leaving work without permission, 37-41
• • emergency leave, declared emergencies, 39
• • family medical leave, 40-41
• • leave provisions under ESA, ensuring compliance with, 37-38
• • • advance notice where possible, 38
• • • discipline prohibited where not possible to give advance notice, 38
• • organ donor leave, 41
• • personal emergency leave, 38-39
• • reservist leave, 40
• off-duty conduct, 58-63
• • criteria, 58

Employee conduct, specific types of *(cont'd)*
• • significant case law: racist and discriminatory beliefs, airing, 58-61
• • • Charter violation permitted by section 1, 58, 59-60
• • • evidence, clear, 60
• • • poisoned environment, 59, 60
• • • specific factors considered, 60
• • • where acquittal, 60-61
• performance issues, 73-76
• • just cause for discharge, requirements for, 73-74
• • • amount of time to improve performance, 74
• • • documenting of performance, 74-75
• • • • follow-up letter, 75-76
• • • • sample letter regarding unacceptable performance, 74-75
• • • minimum performance standards specified and detailed, 74
• • performance appraisals, honest and accurate, 76
• • poor performance treated as non-culpable, 73
• • unionized employees, 75
• • • progressive discipline, 75
• property damage, 48
• sabotage, 48

Employment Standards Act, 2000
• damages arising from termination of employment, 121-123
• • notice of termination, 121-122
• • severance pay, 122-123
• • termination pay, 121-122
• disciplinary records, maintaining, 107
• • *Employment Standards Act, 2000* requirements, 107
• leave provisions under ESA, ensuring compliance with, 37-28, 73
• • advance notice where possible, 37-38
• • absenteeism, 73
• • discipline prohibited where not possible to give advance notice, 38
• • types of leave, 37, 38-41
• • • emergency leave, declared emergencies, 39
• • • family medical leave, 40-41
• • • organ donor leave, 41
• • • personal emergency leave, 38-39
• • • reservist leave, 40
• group benefit plans, 128
• • continued coverage during statutory notice period, 128
• prohibited motives for discipline, 26-27

Employment Standards Act, 2000 (cont'd)
• • discipline prohibited for exercising rights under ESA, 26-27
• • order of employment standards officer, 27
• • rights under ESA, 27

F

Fighting/violence in workplace
• consultation paper, 48-49
• • criminal victimization in workplace, 48-49
• • reasonable precautions taken by employers, 49
• • stakeholders providing input, 49
• cost of workplace violence, 51
• disciplinary letter: suspension for fighting, 85-86
• employee conduct, 51-54
• • physically assaulting manager or supervisor, 51-52
• proposed changes to OHSA, 49-51
• • domestic violence , 50
• • new work refusal procedures, 51
• • risk of violence assessment, 50
• • workplace violence programs, 50-51
• • written policies, 49
• significant case law, 52-54
• • delay in imposing discipline, 52-54
• • "stay of proceedings" not amounting to condonation, 52-53
• • threatening conduct, 52, 53

H

Human Rights Code
• absenteeism, culpable, 71-72
• • attendance management program, unilaterally imposed, 71-72
• • attendance management program, validity of, 72
• arbitrators in union setting having power to apply Code, 31-32
• deemed termination clause in collective agreement, 114-118
• • "negotiated accommodation", 115
• • principles gleaned from *McGill* decision, 115-116
• • whether discriminatory and contrary to human rights legislation, 114-118
• employee conduct, 30
• harassment, sexual and discriminatory, 55
• last chance agreements (LCA), 76-80
• • accommodation, form of, 77
• • drafting considerations, 77-78

***Human Rights Code** (cont'd)*
• • limiting arbitrator's jurisdiction, 76-77
• • significant case law: absenteeism due to alcohol abuse, 78-79
• • • "accommodation" under *Human Rights Act*, 78, 79

I

Insubordination
• unionized environment, 54
• • "obey now — grieve later" principle and exceptions, 54

L

Labour Relations Act, 1995
• complaint vs. civil proceedings, 29
• discipline not to be motivated by anti-union animus, 26
• • factors considered, 26
• proceedings before OLRB, 25-26
• • remedial orders, 26
• unfair labour practices, 25

Last chance agreements (LCA)
• accommodation, form of, 77
• drafting considerations, 77-78
• limiting arbitrator's jurisdiction, 76-77
• significant case law: absenteeism due to alcohol abuse, 78-79
• • "accommodation" under *Human Rights Act*, 78, 79

Leaving work without permission
• disciplinary letters, 86-87
• • suspension for unauthorized absence from work, 86-87
• • warning for unauthorized absence from work, 86
• employee conduct, 37-38
• • leave provisions under ESA, ensuring compliance with, 37-38
• • • advance notice where possible, 38
• • • discipline prohibited where not possible to give advance notice, 38

O

Occupational Health and Safety Act, 35
• complaint with OLRB, 35
• • where disciplined contrary to OHSA, 35

Overview
• constructive dismissal, v
• • fundamental change, v
• • repudiation of contract, v
• disciplinary system, reasonable and transparent, v
• non-unionized workplace, v
• proof of incidents of misconduct, v
• unionized workplace, v

P

Progressive discipline
- disciplinary penalties involved in progressive discipline, 3-6
- • demotions, 5-6
- • dismissal, 6
- • suspensions without pay/final warnings, 4-5
- • verbal warnings, 3
- • written warnings, 4
- non-unionized workplace, 2-3
- • constructive discipline, 2-3
- unionized workplace, 2

U

Unionized employees
- absenteeism, culpable, 71-72
- • attendance management program, unilaterally imposed, 71-72
- • attendance management program, validity of, 72
- collective agreement clauses, 109-118
- • introduction, 109
- • sample clauses, 109-118
- • • deemed termination, 114-118
- • • just cause, 109
- • • non-discrimination clause, 113-114
- • • personnel files, reviewing, 111-112
- • • reasons, issuing, 111
- • • sunset clauses, 112-113
- • • timeliness, 110
- • • union representative, presence of, 110-111
- damages arising from termination of employment, 120
- disciplinary records, maintaining, 106-107
- • *Employment Standards Act* requirements, 107
- • grievance files, 106-107
- • *res judicata*, doctrine of, 106-107
- • sunset clauses, 107
- factors influencing discipline/discharge, 19, 20, 24
- • collective agreement or employment contract, 20
- • status of employee as union official, 24
- *Human Rights Code*, 31-32
- • arbitrators in union setting having power to apply Code, 31-32
- insubordination, 54
- • "obey now — grieve later" principle and exceptions, 54
- *Labour Relations Act, 1995*, 25-26
- • discipline not to be motivated by anti-union animus, 26
- • • factors considered, 26
- • proceedings before OLRB, 25-26

Unionized employees *(cont'd)*
• • • remedial orders, 26
• • unfair labour practices, 25
• last chance agreements (LCA), 76-80
• • accommodation, form of, 77
• • drafting considerations, 77-78
• • limiting arbitrator's jurisdiction, 76-77
• • significant case law: absenteeism due to alcohol abuse, 78-79
• • • "accommodation" under *Human Rights Act*, 78, 79
• *Occupational Health and Safety Act*, 35
• • complaint with OLRB, 35
• • • where disciplined contrary to OHSA, 35
• unionized workplace, v

W

Workplace Safety and Insurance Act, 1997, 35-36